What a refreshing change to find a readin
as four individual performances of the Jesus tradition, yet gives us scope for assessing their combined imaginative impact on the earliest Christian communities.

Meticulously positioned within the discipline of narrative criticism, Cassidy's fine study of Peter in the fourfold Gospel tradition highlights the crucial role played by this imperfect disciple in all four canonical Gospels, and brings to the fore the "sheer gratuitousness" of Peter's call and his "justification by grace."

Dr. Loveday Alexander
Professor of Biblical Studies
University of Sheffield, United Kingdom

This narrative-critical reading of the figure of Peter in each of the four Gospels offers a refreshingly different way into the Gospel narratives. Especially novel is the experiment in "reception criticism." Presupposing that the Gospels were all written for general circulation around the churches, Cassidy asks how each Gospel's protrayal of Peter would have been received in the church at Philippi. Students and others will find this a very accessible and also thought-provoking approach to the Gospels and their early readers.

Dr. Richard Bauckham, F.B.A., F.R.S.E.
Professor of New Testament Studies and
Bishop Wardlaw Professor
St. Mary's College, University of St. Andrews
St. Andrews, Scotland

Is Peter Catholic, or Protestant, or Jewish, or . . .? Richard Cassidy sketches a picture in his book beyond every confessional claim. He looks at the figure of Peter with the eyes of the four Evangelists—from four complete independent and original perspectives. But not enough: in the end he puts himself in the place of a Pauline community in Macedonia, which comes to know the texts of the four Gospels step by step. For us today that means a fifth time Peter: everybody encounters the fisherman from Galilee in his or her own world and context.

Professor Christfried Böttrich
Theologische Facultät
Ernst- Moritz- Arndt- Universität
Greifswald, Germany

Four Times Peter is a window into the construction of the character of Peter in each of the four Gospels and a fascinating reconstruction of how the Gospels might have been read at Philippi. By focusing on each Gospel in turn Richard

Cassidy draws out the character of Peter from each narrative context with striking clarity. This book lends itself to use in both classes and discussion groups because it invariably raises provocative questions about the nature of the Gospels and the ways in which they were read in the early church.

Dr. R. Alan Culpepper
Dean, McAfee School of Theology
Mercer University

This engaging book will lead unsuspecting students through a careful study of the Gospels using narrative criticism, social-world analysis, and theological interpretation while they are having so much fun that they won't realize this is "homework."

Once again, Cassidy has demonstrated his ability to combine narrative criticism, social-world analysis, and theological interpretation to make the study of the New Testament attractive and engaging to readers.

Dr. Sharyn Dowd
Associate Professor of Religion
Baylor University

Richard Cassidy once again demonstrates his skills as a careful reader of texts and an engaging and effective teacher. By approaching the figure of Peter from the perspectives of narrative criticism and reception history, he casts new light on Peter and on each of the four Gospels. In doing so he makes the New Testament come alive in both the 1st- and the 21st-century settings.

Daniel J. Harrington, S.J.
Professor of New Testament
Weston Jesuit School of Theology

The understanding of the figure of Peter in the Gospels is confessionally overloaded. The only way to have a fresh look is to perform a close reading of the texts. Richard Cassidy has good tools to do that: narrative criticism and reception history. His book is clever, nice to read. It gives new insights about this great figure among the disciples of the Nazarene.The reception of the four Gospels by the Christian community at Philippi is the final masterpiece of the book!

Dr. Daniel Marguerat
Professeur de Nouveau Testament
Faculté de théologie et de sciences des religions
Université de Lausanne, Switzerland

Using the category of "paradigmatic readers," Richard Cassidy combines insightful narrative-critical readings of the role of Peter in each of the four Gospels with an imaginative recreation of how they might have actually been received by real readers in the Pauline *ekklēsia* at Roman Philippi. A valuable case study in integrative method in Gospel studies, and a thoughtful contribution to the on-going debate about Gospel audiences in the early church.

Dr. Margaret M. Mitchell
Professor of New Testament and Early Christian Literature
The University of Chicago

Richard Cassidy has written a helpful study of the person of Peter, as presented in the New Testament. Adopting bold approaches to the nature of the Gospels and their readership, he develops a reading of Mark, Luke, Matthew, and John that is as attractive as it is challenging. His final speculation on the arrival of the Petrine tradition and then the four Gospels in Philippi is as provocative as it is stimulating.

Francis J. Moloney, S.D.B.
Provincial, The Salesians of Don Bosco in Australia and the Pacific
Melbourne, Australia

In his new work, Richard Cassidy undertakes a fresh look at the apostle Peter in each of the four canonical Gospels, with the assistance of narrative analysis. Insofar as Peter is often portrayed in the Gospels as a representative disciple, all believing readers become involved. Insofar as Peter as a historical person played (and plays) a foundational role, issues of Church leadership are raised. The reception of Peter in a Pauline community, Philippi in Macedonia, is also explored. In an unprecedented appendix, Peter's words are set forth for the reader's reflection. All in all, this work is welcome as a well-informed, contemporary, guide.

Benedict Thomas Viviano, O.P.
Professor of New Testament
University of Fribourg, Switzerland

INTERFACES

Series Editor: Barbara Green, O.P.

Four Times Peter

Portrayals of Peter in the Four Gospels and at Philippi

Richard J. Cassidy

A Michael Glazier Book

LITURGICAL PRESS
Collegeville, Minnesota

www.litpress.org

A Michael Glazier Book published by Liturgical Press

Cover design by Ann Blattner. Watercolor by Ethel Boyle.

1 2 3 4 5 6 7 8

Library of Congress Cataloging-in-Publication Data

Cassidy, Richard J.
Four times Peter : portrayals of Peter in the Four Gospels and at Philippi / Richard J. Cassidy.
p. cm. — (Interfaces)
"A Michael Glazier book."
Includes bibliographical references.
ISBN-13: 978-0-8146-5178-0
ISBN-10: 0-8146-5178-X
1. Peter, the Apostle, Saint. 2. Bible. N.T. Gospels—Criticism, Narrative. 3. Bible. N.T. Philippians—Criticism, Narrative. I. Title.

BS2515.C38 2006
225.9'2—dc22

2006018681

CONTENTS

DEDICATION

To Edmund Cardinal Szoka and Adam Cardinal Maida in appreciation for the significant initiatives each has made to further the life and mission of Sacred Heart Major Seminary.

To the administration, faculty, staff, seminarians, commuting students, and benefactors of Sacred Heart Major Seminary whose gifts and service combine to promote this seminary as a signature theological institution for the Midwest of the United States and beyond.

PREFACE

The book you hold in your hand is one of fifteen volumes in an expanding set of volumes. This series, called INTERFACES, is a curriculum adventure, a creative opportunity in teaching and learning, presented at this moment in the long story of how the Bible has been studied, interpreted, and appropriated.

The INTERFACES project was prompted by a number of experiences that you, perhaps, share. When I first taught undergraduates, the college had just received a substantial grant from the National Endowment for the Humanities, and one of the recurring courses designed within the grant was called Great Figures in Pursuit of Excellence. Three courses would be taught, each centering on a figure from some academic discipline or other, with a common seminar section to provide occasion for some integration. Some triads were more successful than others, as you might imagine. But the opportunity to concentrate on a single individual—whether historical or literary—to team teach, to make links to another pair of figures, and to learn new things about other disciplines was stimulating and fun for all involved. A second experience that gave rise to this series came at the same time, connected as well with undergraduates. It was my frequent experience to have Roman Catholic students feel quite put out about taking "more" biblical studies, since, as they confidently affirmed, they had already been there many times and done it all. That was, of course, not true; as we well know, there is always more to learn. And often those who felt most informed were the least likely to take on new information when offered it.

A stimulus as primary as my experience with students was the familiarity of listening to friends and colleagues at professional meetings talking about the research that excites us most. I often wondered: Do her undergraduate students know about this? Or how does he bring these ideas—clearly so energizing to him—into the college classroom? Perhaps some of us have felt bored with classes that seem wholly unrelated to research, that rehash the same familiar material repeatedly. Hence the idea for this series of books to bring to the fore and combine some of our research interests with our teaching and learning. Accordingly, this series is not so much about creating texts *for* student audiences but rather about *sharing* our scholarly passions with them. Because these volumes are intended each as a piece of original scholarship, they are geared to be stimulating to both students and established scholars, perhaps resulting in some fruitful collaborative learning adventures.

The series also developed from a widely shared sense that all academic fields are expanding and exploding, and that to contemplate "covering" even a testament (let alone the whole Bible or western monotheistic religions) needs to be abandoned in favor of something with greater depth and fresh focus. At the same time, the links between our fields are becoming increasingly obvious as well, and the possibilities for study which draw together academic realms that had once seemed separate is exciting. Finally, the spark of enthusiasm that almost always ignited when I mentioned to students and colleagues the idea of single figures in combination—interfacing—encouraged me that this was an idea worth trying.

And so with the leadership and help of Liturgical Press Academic Editor Linda Maloney, as well as with the encouragement and support of Editorial Director Mark Twomey, the series has begun to take shape.

Each volume in the INTERFACES series focuses clearly on a biblical character (or perhaps a pair of them). The characters from the first set of volumes are in some cases powerful—King Saul, Pontius Pilate—and familiar—John the Baptist, Joseph; in other cases they will strike you as minor and little-known—the Cannibal Mothers, Herodias. The second "litter" I added notables of various ranks and classes: Jezebel, queen of the Northern Israelite realm; James of Jerusalem and "brother of the Lord"; Simon the Pharisee, dinner host to Jesus; Legion, the Gerasene demoniac encountered so dramatically by Jesus. In a third set we find a similar contrast between apparently mighty and marginal characters: the prophet Jonah who speaks a few powerfully efficacious words; and Ben Sira, sage in late second temple Judah; and less powerful but perhaps an even greater reading challenge stand Jephthah's daughter and Ezekiel's wife. The fourth cluster features the prophet Jeremiah, the northern king Ahab, and the apostle Peter. In any case, each of them has been chosen to open up a set of worlds for consideration. The named (or unnamed) character interfaces with his or her historical-cultural world and its many issues, with other characters from biblical literature; each character has drawn forth the creativity of the author, who has taken on the challenge of engaging many readers. The books are designed for college students (though we think suitable for seminary courses and for serious Bible study), planned to provide young adults with relevant information and at a level of critical sophistication that matches the rest of the undergraduate curriculum.

In fact, the expectation is that what students are learning in other classes of historiography, literary theory, and cultural anthropology will find an echo in these books, each of which is explicit about at least two relevant methodologies. It is surely the case that biblical studies is in a methodology-conscious moment, and the INTERFACES series embraces it enthusiastically. Our hope is for students to continue to see the relationship between their best questions and their most valuable insights, between how they approach texts and what they find there. The volumes go well beyond familiar paraphrase of narratives to ask questions that are relevant in our era. At the same time, the series authors also have each dealt with the notion of the Bible as Scripture in a way condign for them. None of the books is preachy or hortatory, and yet the self-implicating aspects of working with the revelatory text are handled frankly. The assumption is, again, that college can be a good time for people to reexamine and rethink their beliefs and assumptions, and they need to do so in good company.

The INTERFACES volumes all challenge teachers to revision radically the scope of a course, to allow the many connections among characters to serve as its warp and weft. What would emerge fresh if a Deuteronomistic History class were organized around King Saul, Queen Jezebel, and the two women who petitioned their nameless monarch? How is Jesus' ministry thrown into fresh relief when structured by shared concerns implied by a demoniac, a Pharisee, James—a disciple and John the Baptist—a mentor? And for those who must "do it all" in one semester, a study of Genesis' Joseph, Herodias and Pontius Pilate might allow for a timely foray into postcolonialism. With whom would you now place the long-suffering but doughty wife of Ezekiel: with the able Jezebel, or with the apparently celibate Jonah? Or perhaps with Herodias? Would Jephthah's daughter organize an excellent course with the Cannibal Mothers, and perhaps as well with the Gerasene demoniac, as fresh and under-heard voices speak their words to the powerful? Would you study monarchy effectively by working with bluebloods Ahab and Saul, as they contend with their opponents, whether John the Baptist, Peter, or Pontius Pilate? What words of consolation and alarm might Jeremiah offer? Depending on the needs of your courses and students, these rich and diverse character studies will offer you many options.

The INTERFACES volumes are not substitutes for the Bible. In every case, they are to be read with the text. Quoting has been kept to a minimum, for that very reason. The series is accompanied by a straightforward companion, *From Earth's Creation* to John's *Revelation: The INTERFACES Biblical Storyline Companion,* which provides a quick overview of the whole storyline into which the characters under special study fit. The companion is available gratis for those using two or more of the INTERFACES volumes. Already readers of diverse proficiency and familiarity have registered satisfaction with this slim overview narrated by biblical Sophia.

The series challenge—for publisher, writers, teachers, and students—is to combine the volumes creatively, to INTERFACE them well so that the vast potential of the biblical text continues to unfold for us all. These volumes offer a foretaste of other volumes currently on the drawing board. It has been a pleasure to work with the authors of these volumes as well as with the series consultants: Carleen Mandolfo for Hebrew Bible and Catherine Murphy for New Testament. It is the hope of all of us that you will find the series useful and stimulating for your own teaching and learning.

Barbara Green, O.P.
INTERFACES Series Editor
May 16, 2006
Berkeley, California

CHAPTER ONE

Aspects of Narrative Criticism and the Four Gospels

Because Peter appears in the Gospels as a significant figure in Jesus' ministry, and in other parts of the New Testament as a significant figure within the early Christian movement, a large corpus of studies has been devoted to him, including many works analyzing the letters that bear his name.[1] Why, then, a new study of Peter? And why a study of Peter that is restricted in scope to the four canonical Gospels? The basic response to these questions is that this study will employ insights derived from narrative criticism (especially regarding Peter's role within the plot of each Gospel) in treating the four Gospels and, as a consequence, new perspectives regarding Peter will emerge.

1. Aspects of Narrative Criticism

Narrative criticism is not practiced in the same way by every interpreter, but fundamentally it can be understood to encompass three interrelated strategies of analysis. First, narrative criticism seeks to analyze the various elements that serve as building blocks for the overall story the author has narrated. Second, it undertakes to analyze the literary techniques the author employed as a means of presenting the narrative in a coherent and engaging way. Third, narrative criticism investigates the author's assumptions about the readers for whom the story was originally intended. Finally, as a corollary to this last strategy, narrative criticism also pays attention to the context in which present-day readers of the story are themselves actually reading the story.

In analyzing the "building blocks" of a story, narrative critics commonly focus on such elements as character, plot, time, and setting. These elements are present in virtually every narrative and establish the character of the narrative.[2]

In addition to analyzing these narrative building blocks, narrative critics also analyze the literary techniques that authors use to facilitate the presentation of their stories. In this dimension of their analysis narrative critics commonly focus on the overall structure that an author creates as well as other devices such as repetition and inclusion that he or she may use to underscore particular points and to promote overall coherence.[3] In the chapters that follow, the elements of plot, character, time, and setting, along with the literary device of structure, will have particular consequence for the analysis to be presented. It is thus useful to discuss these five aspects now and to provide some sense of how each of them pertains to the interpretation of the Gospel portrayals of Peter.

Concerning character, it should be emphasized immediately that, in all the Gospels, Jesus is the character who dominates. Fundamentally, from beginning to end, each Gospel is Jesus' story. Nevertheless, after Jesus, Peter plays the most important role in terms of the plot of each of the Gospels.[4] As a consequence, any study of a particular Gospel that treats Peter only within the larger group of Jesus' disciples will inevitably fall short in its effort to chart the plot of that Gospel.

What does a Gospel indicate regarding such aspects as Peter's location, family, and occupation? What traits does Peter display? Is he bold? Is he fearful? Is he cowardly? Is he loyal? Is he repentant? What is the quality of his relationship with Jesus? Does he struggle for faithfulness? Does he grow in recognition of Jesus' identity and mission as the story unfolds?

Each evangelist frequently identifies Peter by name and describes his conduct and his interactions in a variety of scenes. As documented in the appendix of this study, in each Gospel Peter speaks far more frequently than any other character except Jesus. Aspects of Peter's character are thus disclosed both by what the evangelist tells about him and also by what Peter "shows" when he himself speaks.

While some of these aspects of Peter's character are illuminated as each Gospel proceeds forward, the four evangelists are more interested in delineating Peter's functioning within the plot of the Gospel than they are in developing him as a character. In other words, because the Gospels are strongly "plot driven,"[5] each evangelist is principally concerned with how Peter advances or hinders Jesus' mission and what Jesus *intends* for Peter. Each Gospel accords substantial attention to Peter, but the focus of each narrative is on the ways in which he variously furthers and frustrates Jesus' objectives.

What, then, is meant by plot? Fundamentally, plot concerns what happens in the story. It is the "unifying structure" that binds the characters and events of the story into a coherent whole. Alternatively, plot is the *intelligibility* that emerges from the interactions of the characters, events, settings, and time in the narrative.[6] Plot regards the "causal logic" that is involved in a story.

In each Gospel Jesus chooses disciples and experiences hostility from various enemies as he pursues his mission.[7] What does he initiate? What happens to him? What happens to his disciples? In what ways does Peter contribute to the furtherance of Jesus' mission? These questions all pertain to the element of "plot."

In addition to character and plot, "time" is a third important element the evangelists use in presenting their stories. It is important at the outset to distinguish between "text time" and "story time." Text time is simply the time required to read a Gospel from start to finish, word by word. Story time refers to the time patterns within the story world of the Gospel.[8] For example, in the Gospel of John, what is the temporal sequence of events in Jesus' ministry and how long does each stage of ministry endure?

The foreshadowing of events is a second aspect of time that is important in all the Gospels. *Prolepsis* is the technical term for this practice of foreshadowing. With respect to Peter's role, "prediction" is the type of *prolepsis* that is particularly important. When Jesus makes predictions that will come to fulfillment before the Gospel narrative ends, such as his predictions of Peter's denials, these are instances of "internal predictive prolepsis." In contrast, when Jesus makes a prediction that will only be fulfilled after the narrative of the Gospel has ended, that is an instance of "external predictive prolepsis."[9] (An example of external predictive prolepsis in the Gospel of Mark is the angelic young man's prediction at Mark 16:7 that the risen Jesus will meet Peter and his other disciples in Galilee.)

What is the time perspective from which each Gospel is narrated? In effect, each evangelist writes from a time location that is after the time of Jesus' resurrection and before the time of his definitive return in glory. The story time of each Gospel principally focuses on the events of Jesus' earthly ministry, with the resurrection events as the final events narrated. Nevertheless, each Gospel indicates that Jesus' definitive post-resurrection return has not yet occurred. The "time of writing" for each of the Gospels is thus located between two temporal events: the event of the Resurrection (a predicted event that has already occurred) and the event of Jesus' definitive return (a predicted event that has not yet occurred).[10]

The immediacy that characterizes each evangelist's manner of narrating is also a feature to note in reflections about "time" and the Gospels. Although decades have elapsed since the events of Jesus' ministry, each of the Gospels portrays these events as though they have only recently occurred. In other words, the Gospels do not narrate the events of Jesus' ministry as though these events pertain to the distant past. Rather, each of the narratives is written with vividness and immediacy to convey that these events are actually quite near and accessible.

The fourth narrative building block used by the evangelists is that of "setting." While types of setting such as clothing (including luminous garments) and artifacts (boats, fishing nets, meal elements, etc.) can have importance for the analysis of particular scenes that appear in a given Gospel, the two most important categories of setting for the purposes of this study are topography and architecture.[11] Topographic settings encompass such natural phenomena as lakes, mountains, and regions. In contrast, architectural settings include such humanly-constructed edifices as temples, synagogues, wells, courtyards, and gardens.

While insights regarding "settings" will not prove to be as significant for this study as will several insights regarding "time," some considerations regarding both topography and architecture will prove useful for the interpretation of the portrayals of Peter by Mark and John. For example, in Mark the topographical setting of Galilee significantly brackets Jesus' endeavors on behalf of the reign of God. It is in *Galilee* that Jesus first begins to announce the Gospel and, after his resurrection, the angelic messenger announces that Jesus will begin anew with Peter and his other disciples *in Galilee*.

Within the Gospel of John there are several episodes in which architectural settings involving enclosures prove significant for Peter's portrayal. One example concerns the parallels between the sheepfold described in John 10 and the high priest's courtyard in John 18. In both of these settings Jesus is the Good Shepherd. But what is Peter's role in reference to the Good Shepherd and his sheep?

The literary device of "structure" is also important for the interpretation of Peter's role within the Gospel narratives. Structure refers to the organizational framework each evangelist develops in order to present his story.[12] While there are fundamental similarities in the story of Jesus as each evangelist presents it, the "paradigmatic reader" (about whom, see below) quickly learns that each narrative possesses its own distinctive structure.

As an example of how the structure of a given Gospel relates to its portrayal of Peter, consider the Gospel of Mark. One of that Gospel's major structural features is its separation into two distinct parts. At 8:27-30 the first section of the Gospel ends. At 8:31-33 the second section begins. Jesus, having been acclaimed as the Christ at the end of section one, now, at the beginning of section two, dramatically announces his coming suffering and death. While Mark's principal focus is on the decisive turn Jesus now makes, his portrayal of Peter at this structural divide is also significant. As the first section of the Gospel ends, Peter is the disciple who decisively *acclaims* Jesus. Yet as the second section of the Gospel begins, Peter emerges as the disciple who decisively *rebukes* Jesus!

If the foregoing comments help to illustrate the approach of this study, it remains to indicate that in the chapters below each of the four canonical Gospels will be treated as though it were the only Gospel existing in the world! In effect, within this study the intention is to let each Gospel be pondered as a single gem, a brilliant piece of jewelry that is fully capable of being appreciated in splendid isolation. The production of a given Gospel might aptly be compared to the "production" of a diamond in that varying elements and various "forces" can be understood to be involved. Nevertheless, within this study it is the finished product of the individual diamond, of the four individual diamonds, that is under scrutiny.

To adhere to such an approach will require following a path that diverges from many of the existing methods for interpreting the Gospels. With respect to studies of Peter in the Synoptic Gospels, a common approach has been to compare a given scene of one Gospel with scenes in other Gospels that resemble this scene. Thus, for example, the scene of Peter sleeping at Gethsemane in Matthew's Gospel is frequently analyzed with reference to the scenes of Gethsemane presented by Mark and Luke.

In contrast, within this study a given Matthean scene involving Peter will only be analyzed with reference to other Matthean scenes involving Peter. Luke's Gospel, John's Gospel, and Mark's Gospel will all be approached in the same way. In other words, the principal approach to any scene portraying Peter will be to determine how this scene fits with the overall story of Jesus (and Peter) that *this particular Gospel* is unfolding.

An additional example of how this study centers its focus on one Gospel in isolation from the others can be seen with reference to the topic of Peter's calling in John's Gospel. In John, Peter is the *third* disciple Jesus calls, whereas he is portrayed as the *first* called in all three Synoptic accounts. After observing John's different positioning of Peter's call, more than one scholar has hastened to conclude that the author of this Gospel must be consciously intending to diminish Peter.[13] Given the methodology of the present study, such a purported conclusion must be set aside. When the story of Peter is treated strictly from within John's Gospel, a far different assessment emerges. (See chapter 5 below.)

The present approach also prescinds from all the intensely discussed questions regarding the oral and written sources a given evangelist used in fashioning his Gospel. This means, for example, that within this study there is no supposition that Matthew and Luke possessed a copy of Mark's Gospel when they themselves each began to write.[14] Such a view is held today by the majority of biblical scholars, with a minority holding that Matthew's Gospel was composed first and that Luke and Mark both had the benefit of having Matthew's presentation in front of them. Studies of Peter that are based on the majority view commonly seek to analyze the putative modifications Matthew and Luke introduced when they used Mark's account in fashioning their own respective narratives. For example, any scholar convinced that Luke possessed a copy of Mark will seek to analyze Luke's scene of Peter's denial, at least in part, by emphasizing that Luke has introduced several modifications that make his scene distinct from Mark's.

Not so in the present study. Below, in the chapter on Luke, no reference will be made to Mark's denial scene when Luke's denial scene is analyzed. Nor will there be any suggestion that Mark's version of Peter's denial provides the basis for Matthew's denial scene. It thus emerges that a key feature of the present study is to keep the portrayal of Peter given in each Gospel "hermetically sealed" from the portrayals of Peter in the other three canonical Gospels. Clearly the process according to which each Gospel was composed is a topic well worth investigating. Nevertheless, the strategy of the present study is to set aside considerations about the composition of each Gospel in order to concentrate rigorously on the story regarding Jesus and Peter that each of these Gospels actually presents.

It is perhaps useful to envision each of these Gospels as a finished document on a new codex or a new scroll. The portrayal of Jesus in each scroll, and the portrayal of Peter as related to Jesus, is the proper focus of this study. No focused analysis of the similarities among the four portrayals of Peter will be provided until the final section of this study, and even then the analysis comparisons will be drawn with very broad strokes.

2. The Various Readers/Hearers of the Gospels

In addition to analyzing the elements of the story and the literary techniques each evangelist uses in presenting his Gospel, consideration must also be given to the various readers/hearers each evangelist intends to reach. Each writes out of his own personal allegiance to Jesus and invites his readers to a deep faith in Jesus and a deep commitment to discipleship in Jesus' name.[15] The story presented by each evangelist is thus intended to transform those who read it. Yet what kinds of readers did each evangelist actually have in view as he composed his work?

The paragraphs that follow will treat two principal categories of readers and will also introduce a topic that will be explored more fully in chapter 6, i.e., the reception of each of the four Gospels at Philippi.

The term "paradigmatic readers" has been formulated as a means of identifying readers who bring an extraordinary sensitivity and talent to their reading of the Gospel texts.[16] What are the leading characteristics of such readers? Like other readers and hearers, paradigmatic readers want to learn more about Jesus and about discipleship in his name. However, in contrast to other readers and hearers who have the same desire, paradigmatic readers have a remarkable ability to analyze the subtle narrative features present within a Gospel.

As discussed above, each of the evangelists uses structure, time, and setting in sophisticated ways. The distinguishing talent of paradigmatic readers is their ability to appreciate the evangelists' sophisticated use of such devices within their narratives. Further, by reason of their willingness to re-read a Gospel multiple times, these readers have the capacity to apprehend the light a Gospel's ending sheds on all that has preceded in the narrative.

It is a thesis of the present study that Mark, Luke, Matthew, and John all had at least a minimum number of paradigmatic readers in view as they entered upon the process of composing their respective narratives. In addition to paradigmatic readers, what other readers did each evangelist envision? Here it is important to recall what was said above regarding the principal purposes of each Gospel: to testify to Jesus and to foster discipleship in his name. Is there any group at any location to whom an evangelist does not desire to proclaim Jesus and encourage discipleship in Jesus' name?

In effect, then, each evangelist envisioned audiences that lived well beyond the specific setting in which he was located.[17] This study's approach to audience thus stands in marked contrast to the approach followed by other scholars who seek to read each Gospel for clues about its specific community much in the way that Pauline scholars analyze Paul's letters for clues about the particular local churches to which Paul was writing.[18]

This is not to deny that each evangelist could well have been influenced by the heritage, ideas, concerns, and needs of the community in which he was located. Nevertheless, it is scarcely possible to know with certitude where any of the Gospels was actually composed.[19] Additionally, each evangelist probably envisioned from the outset that those to whom he first presented his Gospel would soon arrange for copies of it to be shared with the other Christian communities that were a part of the developing Christian network.[20]

This study thus posits that each evangelist envisioned two principal categories of readers: (a) paradigmatic readers and (b) a wide spectrum of other readers and hearers. All of these readers, whether paradigmatic or not, desired to know more about Jesus and the implications of discipleship in his name. The two groups differ principally in their talent for detecting the literary subtleties present within each narrative and in their capacity for and commitment to entering upon multiple re-readings of the text. Further, within a Christian community and/or within a network of Christian communities, literate members, including any paradigmatic readers, presumably read texts aloud for the benefit of community members whose method of learning from texts was primarily aural.[21]

But what gradations of prior knowledge regarding Jesus and the movement in his name does each evangelist presume from his readers and hearers? What prior knowledge does each evangelist presume regarding conditions in Roman-occupied Palestine and in the Judaism of Jesus' day? What prior knowledge is assumed regarding Peter's involvement in Jesus' earthly mission and in the Christian movement since the time of Jesus' resurrection?

These questions defy all efforts to answer them precisely. Given the broad audiences they envisioned, how could each evangelist possibly know all the gradations of knowledge about Jesus and Peter possessed by those who would read and hear his work? The step of predicating a wide audience for each Gospel thus necessitates as a corollary the assumption that each evangelist wrote in the recognition that some members of his audience possessed minimal knowledge regarding the context for Jesus' ministry and for the Christian movement after Jesus.

To the degree that some in the evangelist's audience are well informed regarding Jewish institutions, groups, and conditions in Galilee and Judea, they will correspondingly be able to grasp aspects and nuances of the Gospel narrative that may well puzzle audience members who have no prior knowledge of these subjects. To the degree that members of the audience have participated in the local Christian communities that developed after the time of Jesus, they will be able to grasp aspects and nuances in the portrayals of Jesus' disciples (Peter included) that will escape members of the audience who have only recently come into contact with the Christian movement.

How would readers who possessed very little prior knowledge regarding Jesus' Jewish background respond to the coherence and power of each Gospel's narrative? Is it not part of the "achievement" of the Gospels that readers with very little prior knowledge could still comprehend central truths about Jesus (and have important insights regarding Peter) by the time they reached the end of each narrative?

It should be noted here that one feature of each narrative that virtually all members of its audience could readily grasp was Jesus' crucifixion by a Roman governor. Whatever their location within the empire, whether they were paradigmatic readers or individuals who relied on the reading skills of others, all who read/heard the Gospel narratives presumably experienced little difficulty in understanding each evangelist's account of the Roman procedures that brought about Jesus' death.

Indeed, familiarity with these aspects of Roman rule is perhaps the only "reading credential" each evangelist could presume from virtually all members of his audience. While Gentile readers of the Gospels who were far removed from Palestine might experience difficulty in grasping the facets of the Gospels that presume a familiarity with Jewish religious practice and Jewish life in general, there was no group, Gentile or Jewish, who lacked familiarity with the power of the Roman authorities and their signature practice of crucifixion.

In addition to conjecturing the ways in which members of the original first-century audiences would read or hear the Gospels, narrative criticism also seeks to assess the situation of those reading the Gospel narratives paradigmatically in the twenty-first century. In particular, narrative criticism inquires regarding the social situation of those who presume to step forward as public interpreters of these narratives.

In my own case I read each of these Gospels as a trained biblical scholar and as a Catholic professor teaching at a major seminary and graduate school. Like the first-century paradigmatic readers I presume to interpret, I have committed myself to multiple re-readings of each Gospel and have striven to let the light of each Gospel's ending illumine my re-readings. I also read these texts as a citizen of the United States of America, arguably the most powerful political entity since the Roman empire. Further, I read as someone who has kept a file on Peter in the Gospels since the late 1970s, when I became convinced that Peter's *wrong* answer at Matthew 17:24-27 pointed the way to a true estimation of Jesus' approach to Roman taxation.[22]

The readers who constitute the audience for this book are surely located in a great variety of academic, pastoral, and political situations. I now ask whether your own paradigmatic reading of the Gospel narratives corroborates the interpretation I am proposing for each evangelist's portrayal of Peter. Also, does chapter 6 in this study make an adequate assessment of the Pauline and other factors that presumably influenced the reception of the Gospel portrayals of Peter at Philippi?

3. The Sequence and Authorship of the Gospels

As noted above, the analysis presented in this study is not premised on the hypothesis that Mark's Gospel was written first and then served as a source for Matthew's Gospel and Luke's. Under the methodology for this study, the order in which the Gospels appeared on codices or scrolls as finished narratives can be John, Matthew, Luke, and Mark as well as Mark, Matthew, Luke, and John, or any other sequence. Further, the particular time span in which the Gospels were published is not presumed, nor are the intervals that elapsed between the publication of the first Gospel and the second, third, and fourth. Whether they were written at intervals of five years or ten years or whether all of them were finished within a short period of time, four distinctive Gospels did ultimately appear, and that fourfold appearance is of crucial importance for this study.

Who were the human authors of the four canonical Gospels? For the purposes of this study the "author" of each Gospel is the person who fashioned it into its final form so that, in effect, the contents of the scroll could be read or heard by others. In other words, within this book the author of each Gospel is understood to be the person who *finalized* the contents of the Gospel and *authorized* it for circulation. The final author of the Gospel may have been the *sole* author. From beginning to end, an entire Gospel may be the work of only one human author. Nevertheless, because of strongly supported theories positing multiple authors for the Gospel of John, and because of theories positing an extensive editing process for some of the other Gospels, the importance of the final author's role must be stressed.[23]

4. The Structure of This Book

At the center of this study are four chapters analyzing the Gospels in the order Mark, Luke, Matthew, and John. In light of what has been said above regarding methodology, a word about this chapter order is appropriate. Because they consider Mark to have been published first, the majority of biblical scholars would be comfortable with considering Mark's Gospel first. Yet that is not the rationale for beginning this study with an analysis of Mark's portrayal of Peter.

Within this study the sequence of Mark, Luke, Matthew, and John has been chosen for reasons of pedagogy. The assumption here is that beginning with Mark's "sparse" portrayal of Peter and proceeding toward the other evangelists' more complex portraits will facilitate the reader's appreciation for the nuances present in each account.

Although Mark's Gospel has its own complexities, it is distinctive for the spareness with which it portrays Peter. (Again, within the assumptions of this study Mark could conceivably have been the last Gospel to be published.) In comparison with Mark, Luke's portrayal of Peter encompasses more aspects, but it is arguably not as complex as the versions given by the other two evangelists. Matthew and John may be judged as comparably complex in their respective portrayals of Peter. One pedagogical reason for treating John after Matthew is that John's reference to Peter's Roman crucifixion at the end of his Gospel connects logically with chapter 6 and the analysis of Roman sensibilities at Philippi.

A second structural feature of this book that requires an initial comment is the format according to which chapters 2 through 5 are organized. In each of these chapters the sequence of treatment is (a) Jesus, (b) the disciples of Jesus, and (c) Peter. Pedagogical considerations once again influence the decision to structure the chapters in this way.

Because each evangelist is first and foremost concerned with narrating the story of Jesus, beginning each chapter with an exposition of Jesus' story will allow readers of this study to grasp readily that Peter's trajectory is only a "subplot" of the evangelist's primary story concerning Jesus. Further, since important facets of Peter's identity derive from his membership in the Twelve (Mark and Matthew), in the twelve apostles (Luke), and as a member of the circle of Jesus' disciples (John), a treatment of the group of followers into which Jesus calls Peter also appropriately precedes the sections of each chapter that focus directly on Peter.

The role of chapter 6 within this study also requires comment here. This chapter conjectures regarding the arrival of the four Gospels at Philippi and the response of readers/hearers at Philippi to each evangelist's portrayal of Peter. Because Philippi was a Roman colony and because it was also the location of a Christian community founded by Paul, I have selected it as a test case for assessing a minor thesis of this book concerning the first-century reception of the Gospel portrayals of Peter.

Living in the highly Romanized setting of a Roman colony, the Christians at Philippi were presumably familiar with the Roman emphasis on the *cursus honorum*[24] and were assuredly familiar with the horrific aspects of and the profound "shaming" intended by Roman crucifixions. How could the Christians at Philippi fail to have been moved when they encountered Jesus' prediction of Peter's future crucifixion in John 21? Further, as the recipients of Paul's letter to the Philippians, had these Christians not already assimilated Paul's reflections regarding his own looming Roman martyrdom?

As members of a community founded by Paul, the Philippian Christians were also presumably familiar with Paul's own perspectives on Peter. What were these perspectives? The small number of references to Peter that Paul makes in his letters provide a scant basis for answering this question. Still, the Philippian Christians may well have known the views of Peter that Paul expressed in writing 1 Corinthians and Galatians. Thus when the Gospels began to arrive at Philippi, those reading/hearing them for the first time may well have found there were ideas about Peter that required integration with the images of him they had already formed from Paul's reports and writings and from other sources as well.

Again, any "paradigmatic readers" reading the Gospels at Philippi could have plumbed each Gospel for the subtle nuances its narrative contained regarding Peter. Yet even the least sophisticated readers/hearers at Philippi still possessed the capacity to assimilate many of the Gospel facets of the portrait of Peter, such as his betrayal of Jesus and Jesus' just-mentioned prediction concerning Peter's own crucifixion.

The major thesis of the present study is that in writing principally about Jesus each of the four evangelists presents a fundamentally positive portrayal of Peter. The minor thesis of this book is that the first-century readers/auditors at Philippi and elsewhere would themselves have evaluated these four portrayals of Peter as fundamentally positive. In chapter 6 the readers of this book are thus invited to join me in a type of "reception criticism"[25]—that is, in a shared conjecture concerning the response accorded each Gospel's portrayal of Peter at Philippi in the first century.

An alternate way of describing the secondary aspect of this book is to say that it is concerned with the "impact history" (*Wirkungsgeschichte*) of the Gospel texts. As a text primarily concerned with promoting allegiance to Jesus, what influence did each Gospel have on the Philippians' estimation of Peter once it arrived at Philippi?

CHAPTER TWO

Peter in Mark's Gospel: The Risen Jesus Stands by his Man

In analyzing Mark's portrayal of Peter it is important to recognize that Mark's narrative clearly points toward a future that extends beyond the final scene of the Gospel. Accordingly, the first section of this chapter will investigate this feature of Mark's presentation. The second section will then analyze Mark's overall portrayal of Jesus and his mission. Section three will take up the topic of Mark's overall portrayal of Jesus' disciples. Section four, the most extended section of this chapter, will then proceed to a careful analysis of the portrayal of Peter in the Gospel of Mark.

1. The Future-Oriented Character of Mark's Gospel

To appreciate well the portrayal of Peter that Mark presents within his Gospel it is important to value Mark's indications that the stories of Jesus and of Peter do not end with Jesus' death. In 16:1-8, the best attested ending of the Gospel, the risen Jesus does not appear to anyone and does not speak to anyone. Nevertheless, as the following excerpt indicates, the angelic messenger does make it clear that Jesus has indeed risen from the dead. Further, Jesus will appear to Peter and the disciples once they proceed to Galilee:

> And looking up, they saw that the stone was rolled back—it was very large. And entering the tomb, they saw a young man sitting on the right side, dressed in a white robe; and they were amazed. And he said to them, "Do not be amazed; you seek Jesus of Nazareth, who was crucified. He has risen, he is not here; see the place where they laid him. But go, tell his disciples and Peter that he is going before you to Galilee; there you will see him, as he told you." And they went out and fled from the

> tomb; for trembling and astonishment had come upon them; and they said nothing to anyone, for they were afraid. (Mark 16:4-8)

In effect this passage fulfills numerous instances of internal predictive prolepsis and also functions in terms of external predictive prolepsis. (Recall the discussion of these facets of time in chapter 1.) The angelic message represents the fulfillment of five predictions and allusions regarding his resurrection that Jesus made earlier in the narrative (8:31c; 8:38b; 9:9; 9:31b; 10:34). The crucified Jesus is indeed risen! Further, the messenger indicates the proximate fulfillment of the second part of Jesus' Last Supper prediction regarding his intention of gathering with the disciples in Galilee (14:28): "But after I am raised up, I will go before you to Galilee." Although this gathering is to occur in the proximate future, it is nevertheless projected to take place beyond the ending of the Gospel. For this reason, these words by the angelic messenger should also be regarded as an instance of external predictive prolepsis.

Within the dynamic of Mark's narrative the fearful astonishment that the women at the tomb initially manifest is not a sufficient obstacle to prevent this promised reunion from being accomplished.[1] Jesus and the heavenly messenger have both predicted a future for Peter and the disciples in Galilee, and the consistency of Mark's narrative regarding the fulfillment of Jesus' *internal* predictions argues that this *external* prediction will also soon come to pass.

2. Jesus and his Mission According to Mark[2]

Significantly, the narrator gives his readers two fundamental truths about Jesus in the very first verse of the Gospel. These two truths about Jesus are not effectively grasped by other human characters in the Gospel until after Jesus' crucifixion, and even at that point their appreciation is only implied. What are these two fundamental truths about Jesus? In 1:1 Mark indicates to his audience that he is writing the good news of "Jesus Christ, the Son of God." Both aspects, *Christ* and *Son of God*, are fundamental identifications for Jesus. As Mark's narrative moves forward, Jesus' disciples struggle to comprehend what Mark's readers have already learned, at least incipiently, from the Gospel's very beginning.

Within the Gospel of Mark, what is the nature of Jesus' mission? Although generalization entails certain risks, Jesus' mission can be delineated with reference to the two principal aspects of his identity that have just been referenced. Jesus' identity as Son of God is connected to his mission on behalf of "the reign of God." The second dimension of Jesus' mission is tied to the particularity of his identity as a suffering Messiah. Because Mark does not allude to Jesus' suffering until 8:31 of the Gospel and because he introduces the topic so decisively at that point, it is useful to regard this verse as initiating a new section of the Gospel. As a consequence Part I extends from 1:1 to 8:30 and Part II from 8:31 to 16:8.

In Part I, Mark depicts Jesus taking up the mission path of John the Baptist. Thus, coming into Galilee after his baptism and after his temptation by Satan, Jesus proclaims (1:15): "The time is fulfilled, and the reign of God is at hand; repent, and believe in the Gospel." In addition to proclaiming the reign of God, Jesus also used parables to teach about it. Jesus shares the deeper meaning of these parables with the various disciples whom he calls. For others who remain on the "outside," this deeper meaning remains hidden.

Another key feature of Jesus' reign-of-God ministry in Mark resides in his successful attacks against the forces of evil in their various dominions. In his initial chapters Mark repeatedly portrays Jesus healing human beings and liberating them from possession by demons and evil spirits. Significantly, Mark reports that the demonic spirits Jesus confronted all knew his exalted identity as the Son of God.

Nevertheless, in keeping with Jesus' desire to conceal his identity from humans until he discloses the astonishing truth regarding his coming suffering, these demons, as well as many of the humans freed from demonic influence, are forbidden to testify to Jesus' exalted standing. Mark presents this pattern with such frequency that this "messianic secrecy" motif has come to be recognized as one of his leading narrative strategies.

In Part I of the Gospel Mark also portrays Jesus decrying the legalism and hardness of heart of the Pharisees. Here too, Jesus testifies to, and advances, the reign of God. In Galilee and beyond, Jesus ministers positively in witness to the expansiveness and inclusiveness of the reign of God. His ministry on behalf of tax collectors and sinners and his healing and feeding miracles for Gentiles as well as Jews establish that, in principle, people from all backgrounds are welcome, and provided for, in the reign of God.

The scene in which Peter identifies Jesus as the Christ is highly significant for the structure and plot of Mark's Gospel. In effect this is the final scene of Part I. What transpires in this scene opens the way for Jesus' disclosure in Part II of his path to suffering and death.

When Mark's paradigmatic readers re-read the entire Gospel, bearing in mind the way in which Jesus conducts himself in Jerusalem and the way in which he experiences suffering and death, it becomes clear that Mark has never envisioned Jesus as a triumphant, militarily decisive Messiah. Nevertheless, in Mark's portrayal, Jesus consciously withholds from human beings any disclosure that he is the Messiah until the time when he is prepared to reveal that his messiahship will involve suffering and death.

Viewed from this perspective there is great significance in Peter's role as the first human to identify Jesus as the Messiah. Immediately after Peter's confession, Jesus begins to speak of the suffering and death he will embrace. Indeed, in Part II of the Gospel Jesus repeatedly predicts his suffering and death (8:31; 9:31; 10:33-34) and then experiences the fulfillment of these predictions. In presenting Jesus' embrace of this new dimension of his mission, Mark also portrays him enunciating the view that the sacrificial giving of his life will prove salvific for others (10:45; 14:24).

Although Mark now begins to emphasize Jesus' mission as the Messiah who suffers, he continues to portray him as an agent on behalf of the reign of God, in particular as someone who confronts and challenges those who are opposed to this reign. In Part II Jesus' principal opponents are the chief priests, who are the administrators of the Temple in Jerusalem.

Mark portrays Jesus arriving ceremoniously in Jerusalem and proceeding directly to the Temple, where he surveys "everything" (11:11). The next day, after prophetically cursing a fig tree, Jesus enters the Temple and publicly disrupts its activities, hurling the indictment that "you [the chief priests and scribes] have made it [the Temple] a den of robbers" (11:17).

Within the framework of Mark's narrative this challenge and Jesus' subsequent indictment of the chief priests as "wicked tenants" who have usurped and abused their positions of trust (12:1-11) are the events that galvanize the chief priests to undertake lethal action against Jesus. Aided by Judas' betrayal, they initiate a series of stratagems and manipulations that ultimately result in Jesus' brutal humiliating crucifixion at the hands of the Roman governor. In Mark's narrative, at the point of Jesus' death his entire mission on behalf of the reign of God has seemingly resulted in failure. The great achievements profiled in Part I of the Gospel now seem to recede from the horizon. In undertaking to confront the chief priests and their allies as enemies of God's reign, Jesus seems not to have reckoned with the power of evil. Yet, as has been noted above, those re-reading Mark's account can gain the insight that in some way Jesus anticipates this outcome.

In the final scenes of his Gospel Mark does indeed narrate a harsh *penultimate outcome* for Jesus. This outcome is replete with scorn and beating at the hands of the chief priests and brutal whipping, spitting, and derision from the Roman soldiers. (It will be shown below how the betrayal, denial, and flight of Jesus' disciples intensifies this harshness.) The *ultimate outcome*, however, is God's saving intervention whereby Jesus is brought to resurrected life and future engagement with Peter and his other disciples. In effect, through the Resurrection of Jesus the reign of God has prevailed. This great victory, seemingly in jeopardy until the final verses of the narrative, represents Mark's final perspective on Jesus as Son of God and Christ.

3. The Disciples of Jesus in Mark

Mark records Peter's spoken words in six scenes, and in two of these scenes Peter speaks twice (14:29, 31; 14:68, 71). Simply on the basis of the frequency of his spoken words, Peter must be considered Jesus' most prominent disciple. Nevertheless, Mark does not portray Peter as an isolated follower of Jesus, but rather as part of a group of disciples whom Jesus calls. It is thus appropriate to approach Mark's portrayal of Peter through an analysis focused on the larger group of disciples whom Jesus calls to accompany him.

A. *The Initiative of Jesus in Choosing his Disciples*

It is useful to emphasize from the outset that Jesus is the one who chooses his disciples; they are not the ones who choose him. Thus Jesus authoritatively addresses Simon and Andrew (1:17): "Follow me and I will make you become fishers of human beings." In a similar fashion he authoritatively calls James and John (1:19-20) and later Levi (2:14). Finally in a mountain setting Jesus decisively constitutes a group of twelve disciples to be closely associated with him (3:13-19).

B. *The Role of the Twelve*

The Twelve are thus a group of Jesus' own choosing. According to Mark's narrative, for what purposes does Jesus choose them? Two passages early in Mark's Gospel shed the most direct light on the role of the core group. In describing the formal calling of the Twelve in a mountain setting in Galilee, Mark indicates that Jesus called them for three purposes (3:14-15): (a) "to be with him, (b) "to be sent out to preach," (c) "and to have authority to cast out demons." Subsequently, after his own ministry in Galilee has progressed, Jesus calls the Twelve and begins to send them out two by two, giving them authority over unclean spirits (6:7) as well as other travel instructions. Mark's summary of how the Twelve conducted this mission provides an additional sense of the purposes Jesus initially envisioned for them:

> So they went out and preached that people should repent. And they cast out many demons, and anointed with oil many that were sick and healed them. (6:12-13)

C. *Evaluating the Performance of the Twelve in Mark, Part I*

The verses just cited cast a highly positive light on the Twelve with respect to their performance of the mission Jesus entrusted to them. And what Mark portrays just a few verses later probably confirms that the Twelve performed this mission well. After the disciples return and report to Jesus regarding what they did and taught, Jesus responds to them (6:31): "Come away by yourselves to a lonely place, and rest a while."

Another positive aspect of the disciples' performance is that, at the outset, Simon, Andrew, James, John, and Levi all respond without hesitation to Jesus' call. They literally leave their home surroundings to begin traveling with Jesus, a step that is presumably lauded in Jesus' words at 10:29-30. Throughout Galilee and into Jerusalem they remain "on the way" with Jesus. In the first part of the Gospel (that is, until 8:31 when Jesus begins to speak of his suffering and death), the disciples follow faithfully after Jesus as his ministry on behalf of the reign of God takes him repeatedly to Gentile territories on the other side of the Sea of Galilee and even to the region around Tyre and Sidon. Nevertheless, even in the first part of the Gospel the disciples exhibit serious deficiencies, most especially in their failure to grasp all that Jesus expects them to understand.

"Hardness of heart" is one of Mark's literary motifs and a brief consideration of the three instances in which this concept appears in the first half of the Gospel serves to indicate the seriousness of the disciples' initial failures. At 3:5, in describing Jesus' response to the lack of compassion evidenced by a group of Pharisees for a man with a withered hand, Mark relates that Jesus "looked around at them with anger, *grieved at their hardness of heart*." (After Jesus' healing of the crippled man, the antagonism of these Pharisees is so great that they try to find a way to destroy Jesus.)

Three chapters later, Mark again employs this term. Now it is not criticism for Jesus' enemies the Pharisees, but rather for Jesus' presumed allies, his own disciples! Commenting on the disciples' failure to grasp the significance of Jesus' wondrous feeding of the five thousand and the significance of his walking over water toward the disciples' boat, Mark explains (6:52): ". . . they did not understand about the loaves, *but their hearts were hardened*." Up to this point the disciples are seemingly in a privileged position compared to those "outside," to whom everything is presented in parables (4:11). Now, however, the disciples themselves are being portrayed as though they too are on the "outside."

In the third instance Mark portrays Jesus himself using this term to upbraid the disciples. Jesus has now wondrously provided for the feeding of four thousand on the Gentile side of the Sea of Galilee. Nevertheless, the significance of the fact that Gentiles are now endorsed along with Jews completely eludes the disciples. On their voyage back to the western side of the lake Jesus castigates them with a series of seven staccato-like questions (8:17-21). Especially significant within this series is the third indicting question (8:17c): *"Are your hearts hardened?"* The final question is also significant (8:21): "Do you not yet understand?"

D. *Evaluating the Performance of the Twelve in Mark, Part II*

Because Jesus discloses a startling new dimension of his mission at 8:31 it is possible to divide Mark's Gospel into two parts, with Peter's confession at 8:27-30 signaling the conclusion of Part I. If the disciples were only partially successful in meeting Jesus' expectations in the first section of the Gospel, their performance in Part II worsens.

Within Part II, scenes in which the disciples are portrayed in a consistently positive way are hardly to be found. At the Transfiguration (9:2-10) the inner circle of three, and at the Last Supper the larger group of the Twelve (14:17-26) are both portrayed as enjoying favored communion with Jesus. Nevertheless, at the Transfiguration Peter, James, and John are shown to be fearful (9:6) and uncomprehending of Jesus' closing words about the Son of Man's "rising from the dead" (9:9-10). Similarly, at the Last Supper, when Jesus introduces the topic of his betrayal, the disciples are so uncertain of their own commitments that they ask him, one after another (14:19): "Is it I?"

It is instructive to note that after each of Jesus' solemn predictions of his Passion and resurrection one or more of his disciples is immediately shown denying or failing to comprehend this message. In section four attention will be given to Peter's sharp rebuke of Jesus after the first prediction. As regards the second prediction, Mark initially states (9:32): "But they did not understand the saying, and they were afraid to ask him." Mark then accentuates the disciples' incomprehension by portraying them discussing with one another who was the greatest! After bringing them to admit this, Jesus then reemphasizes the criterion of humility by placing a child in their midst and stressing the importance of receiving the lowly.

The response of James and John to Jesus' third prediction is taken from the same cloth as the entire group's response to the second prediction, only now the emphasis is on the high status James and John hope to receive personally. The two brothers actively petition to sit at Jesus' right and left hand "in his glory" (10:37). Implicitly mindful of his looming suffering, Jesus responds that they do not know what they are asking. Hearing this exchange and the other dialogue that ensues, the ten become indignant toward James and John. It is at this juncture that Mark reports Jesus' words emphasizing a service that contrasts with the domination practiced by the rulers of the Gentiles (10:42-44). At the end of this comment Jesus articulates the important truth (considered above in section one) about his own self-sacrifice: that he will give his life as a ransom for many (10:45).

The Twelve, as well as others (including Bartimaeus), follow Jesus on the way to Jerusalem and two of them prepare his entry into the city just as he instructs them to do. Mark reports little activity by the disciples (Peter's comment about the withered fig tree will be discussed briefly below) during the initial days when Jesus protests powerfully at the Temple and verbally jousts with or attacks the chief priests. One positive reference to be noted briefly is that when Peter, James, John, and Andrew question him about the future of the Temple, Jesus provides them with an extended response (13:3-37) in which he encourages them concerning the future persecution they can expect to face.

From the time of the Last Supper forward the conduct of the disciples spirals downward. Judas' first step toward handing Jesus over is narrated by Mark at 14:10-11, and at 14:18-21 Jesus himself discloses that the betrayal will come from one of the Twelve! Equally startling is Jesus' next prediction (14:27) that all of the Twelve will fall away. Remarkably (and very significantly), Jesus couples this shocking prediction regarding his proximate abandonment with a counterbalancing prediction regarding the more distant future (14:28): "But after I am raised up, I will go before you to Galilee." The importance of this prediction has already been emphasized in section one above.

At this juncture Peter forcefully denies the validity of Jesus' prediction that all his disciples will fall away (see below). Here the point to be emphasized is that the disciples, as a group, signal their willingness to die with Jesus (14:31b). As a group the others are not influenced by Jesus' intervening prediction regarding Peter's three denials (14:30), just as Peter himself is not influenced.

At Gethsemane (14:32-41) Jesus takes Peter, James, and John aside from the rest of the disciples, asking them pointedly to "watch." Nevertheless, they sleep and Jesus addresses Peter as "Simon" in reproving them. Judas then arrives with the arresting party from the chief priests. In the ensuing events one of Jesus' disciples (not named by Mark) strikes with the sword. Jesus himself responds to the arresting party only with a word of reproach (14:43-49).

Mark's next statement describing the final event at Gethsemane is highly significant for an overall evaluation of the disciples' performance in Part II of the Gospel. In view of the prior history of the disciples, the conduct

Mark depicts at 14:50 must be regarded as a truly astounding development. What Mark portrays at this juncture is nothing short of complete abandonment: *"And they all forsook him and fled."*

Within the schema of this study Peter's own threefold denial awaits consideration in section four. Nevertheless, the fundamental ending of the "story" of the disciples during Jesus' public ministry has now been reached. None of these disciples henceforth appears during any of Mark's narratives concerning Jesus' trials, execution, and burial. Still, Mark has not yet completed his entire Gospel, and as he brings his full narrative to a close there will yet be provision for these disciples to be with the risen Jesus in Galilee. More will be said about this when Peter's own denials and his final appearance on Mark's stage are considered.

4. Peter during the Time of Jesus' Public Ministry[3]

The task of the present section, and its subsections, will be to analyze the outlook and performance of Peter as the disciple of Jesus to whom Mark devotes the most attention.

A. *The Names of Peter*

Mark's Gospel mentions Simon/Peter twenty-five times.[4] From 3:16 of the narrative it emerges that Simon was given the name "Peter" by Jesus himself. Mark does not provide any explanation regarding Jesus' motive for taking this step. However, once he reports that Jesus had initiated this name change, Mark himself never again refers to "Simon," but always to "Peter." There is only one exception to this practice. At 14:37, after Peter and the sons of Zebedee have failed to keep watch, Jesus reproaches Peter using his original name, saying: "Simon, are you asleep? Could you not watch one hour?" Jesus seemingly underscores Simon's failure by electing not to address him with the "disciple's name" (Peter) he earlier bestowed on him. Mark's paradigmatic readers may well note that this is the only instance in Mark's narrative in which Jesus addresses any of his disciples by name.

B. *Simon/Peter's Portrayal in Part I*

In part I of the Gospel Jesus has just begun to preach authoritatively about the reign of God when he calls two fishermen. Significantly, Mark names Peter as the first recipient of Jesus' call and accords additional attention to Peter when he identifies Andrew as "the brother of Simon." Mark's full statement about Jesus' authoritative call and Peter and Andrew's decisive reply is as follows:

> And passing along by the Sea of Galilee, he saw Simon and Andrew the brother of Simon casting a net in the sea; for they were fishermen. And Jesus said to them, "Follow me and I will make you become fishers of human beings." And immediately they left their nets and followed him. (1:16-17)

Note that, apart from this initial reference, nothing else is said within Mark's Gospel about Peter's occupation. Thus the emphasis of this account is not so much on what Peter was doing as it is on the fact that he *immediately* and *decisively* left what he was doing once he received Jesus' authoritative call. Mark's characteristic phrase, "and immediately," underscores that Peter accepted Jesus' call without any hesitation.

As the narrative continues, the calling of the first four disciples is followed by Jesus' expulsion of a voluble unclean spirit from a man at the synagogue in Capernaum. Next Mark depicts Jesus entering the house of Simon and Andrew (again Peter is named before his brother). The visit is not solely for the purpose of hospitality because there is a person in the house who is in need of healing: Peter's mother-in-law. Mark provides scant background information about this woman apart from her relationship to Peter and her illness. Jesus' response to her need is sovereignly authoritative (1:31): "And he came and took her by the hand and lifted her up, and the fever left her; and she served them." Mark next reports that people from the whole city gathered at the door of the house to ask for healing. Seemingly Peter's house is thus portrayed as a base from which Jesus conducts his initial ministry in Capernaum.

The third passage in which Simon figures is 1:36-37. Jesus has departed to a lonely place for prayer and Mark describes Simon's response in the following way: "And Simon and those who were with him *pursued* him, and they found him and said to him, 'Every one is searching for you.'" Depending on the translation that is made for the original Greek verb in the first clause, there are two contrasting interpretations of the sense of what Mark here portrays regarding Peter. One possible translation is "search for." Another more negative rendering is "hunt down." This latter translation supports the view that, for the first time, Peter is misunderstanding the nature of Jesus' mission. In effect, Peter is pursuing Jesus as a popular and acclaimed Christ.

Whatever the exact valence of Mark's report in this passage, a subsequent section detailing Peter's selection as one of the Twelve (3:13-19) clearly portrays him (and the others) positively. Mark indicates explicitly (3:13b) that these were the disciples "whom Jesus desired," and he specifies the threefold mission Jesus is now entrusting to them. What we should now consider is the twofold means by which Mark characterizes Peter's position.

First, Mark names Peter at the head of this list of the Twelve. Second, as already mentioned, Jesus here bestows a new name on Simon, renaming him "Peter." Why does Jesus take this step? It is a slightly perplexing feature of Mark's report that no explanation is given for this additional name. Perhaps Mark judged that the members of his audience would deduce that the literal meaning of the word "Peter" expressed Jesus' insight regarding something "rocklike" in Peter's stature or character. As noted above, in 14:37 when Peter's behavior is far from "rocklike," Jesus once again addresses him as "Simon."

In addition to placing him first on his list of the Twelve, Mark also includes four passages within his account in which Peter is shown to be a privileged member of a "subgroup" of Jesus' disciples. The first of these passages occurs at 5:35-43, when Jesus brings three selected disciples to witness his restoration of the synagogue ruler's daughter. Why does Jesus select Peter (named first), James, and John as the members of this subgroup? Mark provides no explanation for this phenomenon, but simply and repeatedly portrays it. In the description that follows Mark's forceful words, "no one" and "except," should not escape notice (5:37): "And he allowed no one to follow him *except* Peter and James and John the brother of James."

As previously observed, in Part I of the Gospel the twelve disciples have a degree of success in carrying out the various aspects of the mission Jesus entrusts to them. Nevertheless, on two separate occasions "hardness of heart" is ascribed to them. It is within this framework of positive and negative performance that Peter's "confession" of Jesus' identity takes place.

In many respects Jesus' reference to new requirements for discipleship and the intense "rise and fall" of Peter that occurs in 8:29-33 constitutes a decisive turning point within Mark's overall narrative. It has been indicated in section one above that these verses mark the first time that a human being identifies Jesus as "the Christ." Peter is that human being, and when this entire passage is read carefully, verse by verse, with pauses between the verses, it can be said that he is presented in a stellar role in 8:29, the actual verse of his confession.

As Mark presents the interchange, Peter speaks authoritatively and before any other disciple responds. Mark's portrayal does not indicate whether any others of the Twelve were capable of this identification. Here, clearly, Mark's spotlight is on Peter functioning in a decisive manner, a spotlighting of decisiveness that Mark presents more than once in his narrative. The following excerpt provides the full context for Peter's (momentary) ascendancy:

> And Jesus went on with his disciples, to the villages of Caesarea Philippi; and on the way he asked his disciples, "Who do people say that I am?" And they told him, "John the Baptist; and others say, Elijah; and others one of the prophets." And he asked them, "But who do you say that I am?" Peter answered him, "You are the Christ." And he charged them to tell no one about him. (8:27-30)

As noted previously, the Markan Jesus' mission will involve the sacrificial giving of his life. Within the narrative of Mark's Gospel it is only at this point, when Jesus is ready to instruct his disciples regarding his suffering and death, that he accepts identification of himself as "the Christ." Nevertheless, he still insists sternly that the disciples not disclose to others that "Christ" is a valid identification for him.

It is precisely at this juncture that Mark portrays Jesus embarking on the momentous effort to educate the disciples about his suffering and death. No other topic is introduced into the narrative between 8:30 and 8:32. Also, it should be noted that Mark does not use his favored connecting words, "and immediately" at this point. Mark thus may intend to suggest an interval between the time when Jesus accepted Peter's confession and the time when he began to predict his suffering and harsh death.

On the other hand, Mark may understand that Peter's confession, Jesus' next prediction regarding his suffering, Peter's rebuke of Jesus, and Jesus' castigation of Peter follow one another in close sequence. In this reading Jesus' impassioned upbraiding of Peter completes a four-part series of exchanges that is swift, forceful, and almost literally *stunning*. Bearing in mind these questions regarding the time intervals involved, the verses that now follow 8:30 can now be considered in their entirety:

> And he began to teach them that the Son of man must suffer many things, and be rejected by the elders and the chief priests and the scribes, and be killed, and after three days rise again. And he said this plainly. And Peter took him, and began to rebuke him. But turning and seeing his disciples, he rebuked Peter, and said, "Get behind me, Satan! For you are not on the side of God, but of human beings." (8:31-33)

Regardless of how much time Mark understands between Peter's confession of Jesus and his rebuke of Jesus, it soon becomes clear that Peter's attempted rebuke introduces a major dissonant note into Mark's narrative concerning Jesus and his disciples. This is so even if Mark's readers initially regard Peter's rebuke as well intentioned. Does Peter not have Jesus' safety and success in view? Peter simply wants to dissuade his master from a "lapse" that could cause Jesus to embark upon a treacherous and fatal path.

At this point what is unknown to Peter is that Jesus is uncompromisingly serious in making this prediction. Jesus will indeed experience such a death (and resurrection). Further, the Markan Jesus knows that this very willingness to give his life sacrificially defines his identity as the Christ! And thus does the graveness of Peter's failing become manifest. For Peter is blind to the very heart of Jesus' mission. Since Mark also explicitly indicates that Jesus takes the rest of the disciples into his view when he castigates Peter, it seems certain that the fundamental blindness Mark is portraying is not restricted to Peter alone.

Nevertheless, it is singularly Peter whom Jesus decries as "Satan." If Peter has just been forceful in trying to reprimand Jesus for speaking about suffering and death, Jesus is even more forceful in identifying Peter with the one who is the source of evil and Jesus' chief adversary in the Gospel of Mark.

A consideration of the way in which "Satan" is portrayed in the Gospel of Mark is useful at this point. Before the beginning of his public ministry, when Jesus was in the wilderness for forty days, Satan was the one who tempted him (1:13). Later on in Galilee Jesus endures a frontal attack by scribes from Jerusalem who say that he is possessed by, and authorized by, Beelzebul, the prince of demons. Without denying the power of Satan, Jesus discredits the scribes' charge by pointing out the illogicality of it. If Satan tried to cast out Satan, the result would be Satan's destruction (3:22-26). Later, in explaining the parable of the sower, Jesus credits Satan with an effective power for filching the word of God from those who are not properly prepared to hold it fast (4:15).

Satan's negativity is thus consistently emphasized within Mark's Gospel and now, in 8:33, Peter is said to be functioning as Satan! Peter has egregiously violated his privileged call to follow Jesus in witnessing to the reign of God. Instead, exactly in the manner of Satan, Peter is thinking in a way that is diametrically opposed to "the things of God."

What, then, does Jesus require of Peter at this juncture? "Get behind me, Satan," the words of 8:33, can be interpreted as a stern admonition to Peter to return to his foundational calling. When he decisively called him, Jesus' words to Peter were "Follow me" (1:17). And later on, when Jesus formally selected the members of the Twelve, it was the assigned role of

Peter and the others "to be with him [Jesus]." Peter, then, is to return to his foundational commitment as Jesus' disciple even as Jesus presents Peter (and the others as well) with radical new requirements for their faithful following after him and being with him.

Significantly, Mark does not indicate Peter's reaction, or any response, to the severe upbraiding he has just received from Jesus. What does Peter feel? How does he comport himself after receiving such a severe chastising? What was the reaction of the other disciples at seeing Peter so decisively censured? It is useful to pose these questions in order to underscore what Mark's narrative does *not* disclose.

In contrast with the response Mark will later attribute to Peter after his second major failure (14:72c; see below), it should be emphasized that here Peter expresses neither apology nor repentance. Egregious though this failure may be, Peter does not depart in shame. Instead, the narrative continues with Jesus' own amplification regarding the new situation he has just disclosed. To his disciples as well as to others (8:34a), Jesus begins to elaborate on the topic of giving one's life. He has just disclosed that he will lose/give his own life. Now he indicates that he asks such a commitment from his disciples. The key verse expressing this requirement is as follows: "If any would come after me, let them deny themselves and take up their cross and follow me" (8:34b, *NRSV*).

Given the analysis made in section one concerning Jesus' death on a cross and Simon of Cyrene's role in carrying Jesus' cross, the appearance of the word *cross* in Jesus' explanatory words is extremely significant. What precisely is the meaning that emerges from Jesus' reference to the carrying of a cross?

The cross that is in view here is the Roman cross of crucifixion, the same cross that looms so large at the end of the Gospel. In the preceding verses Jesus prophesies that he will be killed, and it is now obliquely intimated that the "killing" will be through Roman crucifixion. In the third Passion prediction this initial oblique reference will be clarified further by Jesus' indication (10:33-34) that "the Gentiles" will carry out his execution after they *scourge* him. Given these references to whipping and to execution by the Gentiles, it thus emerges that the meaning of "carrying one's cross" is oriented to death by crucifixion.

In effect, then, Jesus is now indicating to his disciples (Peter included) and others that, to follow him with faithfulness, they must be ready to die, ready to suffer death by crucifixion. The cost of discipleship is thus drastically increased! Yet this raised price follows logically from the disclosure of the previous verses that Jesus himself is prepared to suffer rejection and death.

Jesus, in 8:35-38, then establishes the paradoxical wisdom of this stance of giving one's life. Whoever does this for Jesus' sake and for the sake of the Gospel will actually save his or her life. But all who refrain from following Jesus' example will find Jesus "ashamed of them when he comes in the glory of his Father with the holy angels" (8:38c).

Once again it is useful to note that Mark records no response by Peter to Jesus' startling, challenging exposition. Does this exposition help Peter to grasp how inappropriate it was for him to try to rebuke Jesus? Does it help Peter to grasp that, even as Jesus is one who will face an imposed death, so Peter, as Jesus' disciple, is now challenged to be willing to give his own life?

C. *Peter's Portrayal in Part II of Mark*

The account of the Transfiguration follows next in Mark's narrative (9:2-8). Given the focus of this study, the first aspect to be noted is that Jesus' call to Peter as his disciple is now renewed. Jesus is graciously allowing Peter to move beyond the previous episode in which Jesus' words identified Peter as an agent of Satan.

While Jesus' initiative in inviting Peter to share the transfiguration events is important, Peter's acceptance of the invitation is not unimportant. At this point, what is Peter's understanding of Jesus' path? Does Peter now accept that Jesus is indeed heading toward rejection and death? Is such a change in Peter's perspective implicit in the fact that, instead of departing, Peter accepts Jesus' invitation to continue to be with him?

Within the larger framework of Mark's narrative, Jesus' sovereign initiative in selecting Peter to experience the Transfiguration may foreshadow another instance in which Jesus will sovereignly intervene to bring this disciple forward after an even more egregious failure on Peter's part. In effect, Jesus' initiative to renew Peter after Peter's Satanic denial of Jesus' suffering prefigures Jesus' initiative to restore Peter after his terrible denial that he (Peter) even knows Jesus. (See section 5 below for an analysis of this second major initiative by Jesus.)

The transfiguration events wondrously confirm for Peter, James, and John the validity of Jesus' startling, disconcerting teaching that he will suffer and die at the instigation of the chief priests and then rise after three days. The divine voice they hear from the cloud solemnly declares, "This is my beloved Son; *listen to him*" (9:7; emphasis added).

In addition, although the meaning is scarcely comprehensible to them, they are given some sense of the reality of the Resurrection when they view Jesus' glistening, intensely white garments and contemplate his transfigured appearance (9:2-3). They are also given a veiled reference to the Resurrection when Jesus subsequently admonishes them not to speak of their experiences "until the Son of Man should have risen from the dead" (9:9b). Mark adds, though, that they kept questioning among themselves what "rising from the dead" actually meant (9:10).

Overall, Peter's performance at the time of the Transfiguration admits of mixed assessments. Speaking out, Peter reverently expresses gratitude to Jesus: "Master, it is well that we are here" (9:5a). Yet Mark also indicates that "he did not know what to say" (9:6a), suggesting that Peter has misspoken in proposing to Jesus that the disciples construct three booths for Jesus, Elijah, and Moses. Nevertheless, Mark also alludes to the disciples' fear as a fact mitigating Peter's inappropriate proposal. One commendable feature of the disciples' response (Peter's included) is that they do heed Jesus' command to keep all this to themselves until after the resurrection.

What is the sense of Peter's allegiance to Jesus after the Transfiguration? If the key criterion of discipleship is to be "with Jesus," Peter is continuing to meet that criterion. It cannot be ascertained from Mark's next passages whether Peter continues to reject suffering and death for Jesus. Similarly, it cannot be determined from the narrative whether Peter has accepted Jesus' teaching that his disciples themselves must be willing to embrace their own crosses. What can be observed is that Peter now continues with Jesus on the way toward Jerusalem.

Jesus himself goes on teaching that death and resurrection lie ahead, and at 9:33-37 he criticizes the disciples as a group for failing to grasp his meaning. Further, at 10:35-45 James and John are expressly portrayed as missing the meaning of Jesus' words. What is Peter's own attitude at this point? In the not very distant future Peter will show that he no longer considers it unthinkable that Jesus is called to face death.

Prior to the events of the Last Supper there are three additional scenes in which Peter plays a named role. In two of these episodes Peter is the sole speaker. In the third episode he is part of an inner group with James and John and also Andrew. Within this last scene, the question to Jesus seems to arise from all four members of the group.

At 10:28, following Jesus' encounter with the rich man and the disciples' astonishment over Jesus' teaching regarding riches, Peter takes the initiative, asserting, "Lo, we have left everything and followed you." In basically accepting Peter's bold claim, Jesus encourages him for having made this sacrifice. However, note that Jesus' subsequent comment amplifies his words. First, Jesus broadens the frame of reference to take in others as well when he indicates that bounteous rewards will be received (10:29-30a). Second, Jesus indicates that "persecutions" are included in the list of the blessings to be received (10:30b). Third, he adds the assessment that many presently first will find themselves last and those presently last, first (10:31).

At 11:21 Peter again speaks out, alerting Jesus to the fulfillment of his prophetic cursing of the fig tree on the outskirts of Jerusalem. Here Jesus takes Peter's comment as a point of departure in order to address all the disciples regarding the power of faith, the effectiveness of prayer, and the necessity of forgiveness (10:22-25). The final pre-Passover episode in which Peter figures is again a scene in which he is named first among a smaller circle of disciples. In this instance the disciples' question to Jesus about the Temple's destruction elicits an extended response from Jesus (13:4-37). Included within Jesus' remarks is an external predictive prolepsis indicating that "you" (a group in which Peter has been named first) ". . . will be beaten in synagogues; and you will stand before governors and kings for my sake, to bear testimony before them" (13:9b).

Two days later, in the context of the Last Supper and its aftermath, Jesus again twice speaks of the future. In these two instances his words pertain to the near future and represent instances of internal predictive prolepsis. At 14:18 he indicates that one of those *"with me"* at table will betray him. After the supper has ended, he says:

> "You will all fall away; for it is written, 'I will strike the shepherd, and the sheep will be scattered.' But after I am raised up, I will go before you to Galilee." (14:27-28)

Jesus' words in the first part of his statement are speedily fulfilled within Mark's narrative. In effect these first words contrast with the second part of the statement announcing Jesus' intention to proceed to Galilee after his resurrection. This latter prediction is fulfilled only in the second-last verse of the Gospel.[5]

Jesus' prediction that all will desert him thus motivates Peter to contradict Jesus for the second time within the Gospel: "Peter said to him, 'Even though they all fall away, I will not'" (14:29).

Note that Peter's declaration focuses only on the first part of Jesus' prediction, that all will fall away. He does not comment at all on Jesus' reference to being raised up and going before the disciples to Galilee. This is the second time within Mark's narrative that Peter has failed to delve into the meaning of Jesus' words regarding resurrection (recall 9:10), and Mark thus signals to his paradigmatic readers that any grasp of the Resurrection is utterly beyond Peter's capability during the time of Jesus' ministry.

In presuming to contradict Jesus' prediction, Peter exudes self-confidence and also implicitly evidences a sense of superiority. Conceivably the other disciples might not remain with Jesus, but Peter's commitment is so unshakable that *he* will withstand the pressures that might undermine others.

Jesus' response is to declare specifically and concretely that Peter will deny him three times before the cock crows twice (14:30). Within Mark's narrative Jesus' anticipations of his future relate not only to such headline elements as suffering, death, and resurrection. His predictive prolepses also regard highly specific developments; here the reference is to *three* denials taking place precisely before the *second* crow of the cock.

Peter once again boldly contradicts Jesus! His impassioned proclamation is: "If I must die with you, I will not deny you" (14:31a). Setting aside for the moment his inability to live up to this declaration, there are at least two positive aspects represented within Peter's words. The first is that he ardently manifests a desire to be *with Jesus* even in death. This is, in effect, the moment of Peter's highest standing within the Gospel narrative. He is now so personally committed in his allegiance to Jesus that he will readily die *"with you."*

The second positive aspect concerns the significant progress Peter has made in understanding the profound new dimensions Jesus disclosed at 8:31-38. In contrast with his attitude in rebuking Jesus at 8:32, Peter now no longer disputes that Jesus will suffer death, nor does he reject Jesus' counsel that his disciples should be prepared to embrace the cross. In effect, Peter's words at 14:31 indicate a recognition that Jesus may well undergo death; they also indicate his own willingness to be with Jesus in death. Peter's progress, signaled by this bold declaration, is unmistakable. The other disciples' affirmation of Peter's words (14:31b) signals that they too are ready to accept the high standard of discipleship Jesus originally proposed at 8:34-38.

Nevertheless, bold words are not the same as brave deeds, and a deeper evaluation of Peter's discipleship turns on the question whether he will carry out his stated commitment to die with Jesus. Jesus has predicted that *none* of his disciples will remain with him. Will Jesus' prophecy be proved correct, or is there some way in which Peter's bold words will somehow be upheld? As Mark has unfolded the aspects of his narrative concerning Peter he has been successful in engendering among his readers (especially among first-time readers with little prior knowledge regarding Peter) a degree of suspense about this disciple's future.

From Gethsemane onward Peter simply cannot bring forward the principled conduct his own brave words have just avowed. In Gethsemane Peter (as noted previously, Jesus now addresses him as "Simon") and the other disciples repeatedly sleep instead of keeping vigil (14:37-42). At the moment of arrest one disciple does strike with the sword on Jesus' behalf (14:47). However, "all" then precipitously forsake Jesus and flee (14:50). In effect, only hours after Jesus predicts that all will abandon him, his prediction is fulfilled, and Peter is included in the "all."

Nevertheless, this abject failure is not the end of Peter's story in Mark. Indeed, the evangelist now portrays Peter's new attempt to be with Jesus. Jesus is led before the high priest and Peter *"follows him"* right into the high priest's courtyard. However, Peter's "following" is now more tentative than confident. Mark adds the descriptive note that he followed "at a distance" (14:54).

After he describes the Sanhedrin's interrogation of Jesus and the spitting and blows Jesus then received from his guards (14:55-65), Mark shifts his spotlight back to Peter, who has been standing below in the courtyard. It is possible to identify a slight crescendo in the three denials Mark then describes Peter making.

In the first episode the wording of the maid's assertion must be read against the two other Markan texts in which a critical requirement is being "with Jesus." Just verses earlier Peter has vowed his willingness to die "with you" (14:31). Now the maid's reproach is that Peter was "*with* the Nazarene, *Jesus* (14:67b). The words Peter uses to deny this accompaniment have a tautological quality to them (14:68): "I neither know nor understand what you mean."

Peter's exact words in his second denial are not recorded by Mark. This is a more public denial, due to the fact that the maid verbally accosts Peter in front of others who are standing near. The third episode also involves a group of bystanders who posit Peter's association with Jesus because he (Peter) is a Galilean (14:70). Now, dramatically, Peter invokes a curse on himself and swears by oath (14:71): "I do not know this man of whom you speak." Clearly Peter's third denial is presented as a complete distancing of himself from Jesus.

Within Mark's Gospel, Peter's trajectory in following after Jesus and remaining with him is now at its nadir. Only a few hours earlier he proclaimed his willingness to die with Jesus. Now he affirms that he has no ties with Jesus. He does not even know him!

Peter's situation appears even more abject for paradigmatic readers who have the opportunity to reflect again on Jesus' words at Mark 8:34-38. In the aftermath of Peter's "satanic" attempt to dissuade him from the path of suffering, Jesus counseled (8:34): "If any man would come after me, let him deny himself. . . ." Peter has now fully denied, not himself, but Jesus! Further, at 8:38 Jesus spoke of the definitive shaming the Son of Man will enact for anyone "ashamed of me and of my word." In the high priest's courtyard, *speaking his last words within the Gospel*, Peter has now epitomized the meaning of being ashamed of Jesus.[6]

Earlier, when Jesus vehemently rebuked Peter for having tried to dissuade him from the path of suffering (again see 8:33-34), Mark reported neither repentance nor a request for forgiveness by Peter. Peter now behaves in a way that is in marked contrast. After the second cockcrow he "broke down and wept" (14:72c). The full meaning of these words may be that Peter now experiences a desperate sorrow that involves his physical collapse.[7] This portrayal of Peter's anguish should also be viewed within the context of Mark's silence regarding sorrow by any of the other disciples who forsook Jesus and fled.

Mark's report of Peter's profound sorrow over what he has done enables Peter to "rise," if ever so slightly. Nevertheless, it must not be overlooked that, despite his repentance, Peter is no longer *with Jesus*. He is no longer *following Jesus*. Both of these assessments are confirmed in the remaining sections of Mark's Passion narrative. Peter's tears of sorrow do not impel him to Jesus' side for any remaining part of Jesus' sufferings and trials. For example, Peter's sorrow does not impel him to be with Jesus to assist in the carrying of his cross to Golgotha. And even from afar neither Peter nor any of the other members of the Twelve are with Jesus during the harsh hours of his crucifixion.

What will happen to Peter? Once again Mark's narrative engenders a certain suspense regarding the future of this disciple. By reason of his denials of Jesus he is vulnerable to having the Son of Man be ashamed of him. Yet he has shed tears of sorrow and anguish. Still, he does not proceed to Jesus' side and leaves Jesus to face crucifixion and death with nary a word of support. What will happen to Peter?

5. Peter and the Risen Jesus

As noted previously, the Gospel of Mark ends with a strong emphasis on the harshness of Jesus' death and makes only brief reference to the Resurrection.[8] Nevertheless, just as Jesus' previous prediction concerning the flight of all his disciples and Peter's threefold denials are both fulfilled, so now is Jesus' prediction to the disciples at 14:28 also fulfilled.[9] "But after I am raised up, I will go before you to Galilee."

Note again that there are two parts to the prediction and that both of them are confirmed through words of the angelic messenger at the tomb. Confirming the first part of Jesus' prediction, the messenger says (16:6b): "He has risen; he is not here; see the place where they have laid him."

The heavenly messenger also confirms the second part of Jesus' prediction, but his confirmation simultaneously constitutes a new instance of external predictive prolepsis. The disciples have not yet seen the risen Jesus but, as their story continues beyond the end of Mark's narrative, they *will* encounter him once they arrive in Galilee (16:7): "But go, tell his disciples and Peter that he is going before you to Galilee; there you will see him as he told you."

The angel's message to the faithful women explicitly singles out Peter[10] as among those with whom Jesus will reunite in Galilee. This is what will happen to Peter. He is rehabilitated because Jesus' earlier general prediction regarding a post-resurrection reunion with his disciples will now be fulfilled. It is the risen Jesus' desire to fulfill his earlier prediction, rather than any human calculation based on the disciples' performance and Peter's performance, that now proves to be operative.

Because of Jesus' sovereign initiative, Peter, who has failed so abjectly, along with the others who failed just as badly, is now given a mandate for reuniting with Jesus in Galilee. Why is Peter designated by name?[11] Within Mark's account there is a consistency in terms of Jesus' sovereign interventions on behalf of Peter. With full sovereignty Jesus selected Peter as his first disciple, changed his name, visited his home, healed his mother-in-law, and so forth. Now with full sovereignty Jesus sets aside Peter's denials and his blatant failure to be with him at the cross. He decrees through the angel's words that Peter and the others are to be *with him* for a future that begins in Galilee. Possessing the fullness of sovereignty, the risen Jesus intends this future with all his disciples, and according to Mark's ending he intends it, in particular, with Peter.

6. Summary of Mark's Portrayal of Peter

Jesus' three bold initiatives on behalf of Peter are central to Mark's portrayal of this disciple. These initiatives are: initial calling, pre-resurrection restoration, and post-resurrection restoration.

Jesus' call to Simon and his selection of him as a specially named member of the Twelve are both facets of the calling Peter initially receives. Despite several instances in which his performance (and that of the other disciples) is less than satisfactory, Part I ends with Peter at his zenith in confessing Jesus' identity as the Christ. Nevertheless, once Part II opens, Peter plummets precipitously by rebuking Jesus and trying to dissuade him from following the path toward suffering and death. At this point Jesus undertakes his second major initiative on behalf of this disciple. Jesus invites

Peter to be present for the Transfiguration and thereafter to continue to follow him.

Peter's second steep decline occurs as a consequence of his three denials. Despite Peter's public repudiation of him, the risen Jesus once again intervenes on Peter's behalf, signaling that this disciple still does have a future "with him." Mark's account thus ends with these rather stark perspectives: Peter has a future with Jesus and that future will involve persecution.

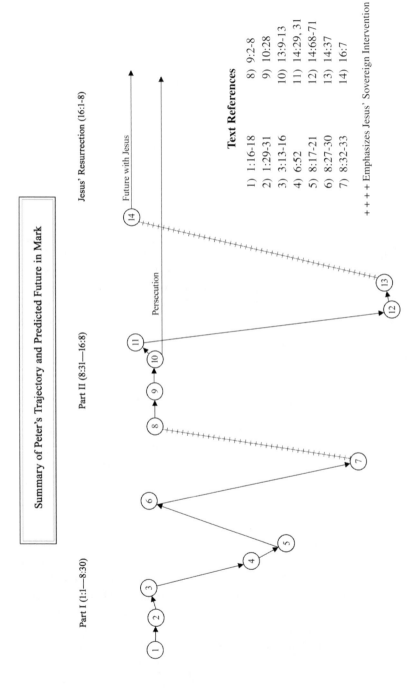

Summary of Peter's Trajectory and Predicted Future in Mark

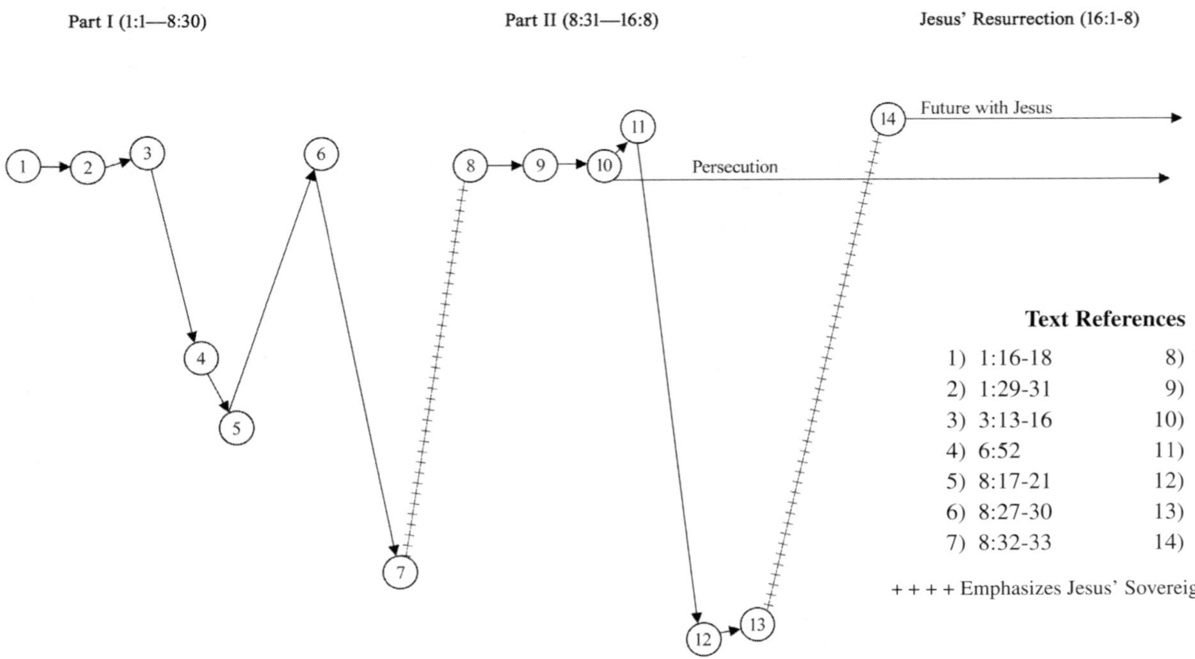

Text References

1) 1:16-18	8) 9:2-8
2) 1:29-31	9) 10:28
3) 3:13-16	10) 13:9-13
4) 6:52	11) 14:29, 31
5) 8:17-21	12) 14:68-71
6) 8:27-30	13) 14:37
7) 8:32-33	14) 16:7

+ + + + Emphasizes Jesus' Sovereign Intervention

CHAPTER THREE

Peter in Luke's Gospel *Praying, Sifting, Turning, Strengthening*

The first section of this chapter will establish that Luke's Gospel projects a future for Peter and the other members of the eleven that extends beyond its final scene. The second section will analyze Luke's presentation of Jesus and his mission in general terms. Section three will then take up Luke's portrayal of Jesus' disciples. Luke's depiction of Peter will then be the subject of sections four and five. Again, the approach of this study is always to treat first Jesus' own ministry and his call/commission to his disciples as a group in order to establish the context for what each Gospel says about Peter.

1. The Future-Oriented Character of Luke's Gospel

Because this study focuses on the portrayal of Peter within the four canonical Gospels, the present chapter will prescind from any investigation of Peter's portrayal in Luke's second volume, the Acts of the Apostles. Luke's Gospel possesses its own cohesiveness as a narrative, and its portrayal of Peter can be analyzed without reference to Peter's post-resurrection discipleship as Luke describes it in Acts.

In section four, seven external predictive prolepses concerning Peter and the eleven will be listed and analyzed. Here it suffices to note that in the final scene of the Gospel Jesus entrusts the disciples with three mandates for the future. At 24:47 he commissions the disciples for the preaching of repentance and the forgiveness of sins to all nations. At 24:48 he credentials them with the words, "You are witnesses of these things." Third, in 24:49a he indicates that he will send "the promises of my Father" upon them.

Luke's Gospel then closes with Jesus' disciples in Jerusalem awaiting the beginning of their future ministry. They are to remain in the city until they are clothed "with power from on high" (24:49b). Once they receive this strengthening power, the way will be open for the endeavors and ministries Jesus has already identified for them.

2. Jesus and his Mission According to Luke[1]

The character of Jesus' mission in Luke must be investigated from the standpoint of significant motifs that occur within his public ministry, but also in light of significant motifs and perspectives that are present in the chapters that precede Jesus' inaugural visit to Nazareth. One way of conceptualizing Jesus' mission in Luke is to view him as the bringer of salvation.

The terms "Savior" and "salvation" are themselves highly useful for characterizing Jesus and his mission in Luke.[2] In indicating to the shepherds the significance of Jesus' birth, Luke's angels say: "for to you is born this day in the city of David *a Savior*, who is Christ the Lord" (2:11; emphasis added). Subsequently, while holding the child Jesus in his arms, Simeon expresses praise and gratitude with the words, "for mine eyes have seen thy *salvation* which thou hast prepared in the presence of all peoples" (2:30-31; emphasis added). When he encounters Zacchaeus during the course of his ministry, Jesus himself declares, "Today *salvation* has come to this house, since he also is a son of Abraham. For the Son of man came to seek and *save* the lost" (19:9-10; emphasis added).

When other Gospel occurrences of "Savior" and "salvation" are considered (Mary's use of "Savior" at 1:47 and Zechariah's testimony regarding "salvation" at 1:69 and 1:77) it becomes still more evident that Luke regards salvation as a central concept. Although the present analysis is intentionally restricted to the boundaries of the Gospel, it is still useful to draw minimal attention to some of the references to "salvation" in Acts. At Acts 4:12 Peter boldly declares: "And there is *salvation* in no one else, for there is no other name under heaven given among people by which we must be *saved*" (emphasis added). "Salvation" is also three times related to the missionary endeavors of Paul in Acts (13:26, 13:47; 16:17). Finally, during the very last scene of Acts, Paul speaks decisively concerning a salvation that is inclusive of Gentiles (28:28).

What is the content of the "salvation" that Jesus brings? Certainly it encompasses healing from various forms of illness. Second, it involves specific affirmation for traditionally less-regarded groups: the poor, the infirm, women, Samaritans, tax collectors. These and other dimensions of salvation appear prominently in Jesus' inaugural proclamation in the synagogue of Nazareth (4:16-30). In this passage there is also an adumbration of the universal character of this salvation, something that contributes to the lethal hostility with which the scene concludes.

This theme of a salvation that provides for the lowly also finds expression in the second noteworthy structural block in Luke's account of Jesus' public ministry, his Sermon on the Plain in 6:17-49. The third important structural feature of Luke's Gospel is Jesus' journey toward Jerusalem (9:51–19:44). During this extended journey Jesus' parables and his healings of various individuals both serve to broaden and specify the nature of the salvation he came to bring.

Who stands in opposition to Jesus and his mission of bringing salvation? This question directs attention to the complex features of the plot in Luke's Gospel and requires two distinct yet complementary responses. The suprahuman opponent of Jesus and his mission is Satan (also referenced as the devil). The primary human opponents are the chief priests of Jerusalem and their allies. The Roman governor and the Roman imperial system are also characterized as being in opposition to Jesus in various ways. For example, Luke will show that the salvation Jesus advances is in sharp contrast with the "salvation" proffered by the Roman authorities.

Not every facet of Luke's plot can be treated here. Nevertheless, with a view to fostering an appreciation for Peter's role within the plot of Luke 22–24 it is important to establish that, as reported in 4:1-13, the devil sought to deter Jesus from his appointed mission even before his public ministry began! Jesus overcame the devil's initial temptations. However, this defeat for the devil does not mean that his opposition ended, for Luke writes at 4:13b that "he (the Satan) departed from him until an opportune time."

Luke 22 will highlight the Satan's re-emergence and, in particular, his demand to "sift" all of Jesus' remaining apostles as he has already sifted Judas. At this stage in Luke's plot Jesus will unveil a strategic response to Satan in which Peter emerges (by reason of Jesus' prayers) as a pivotal figure.

On the plane of human opposition, the salvation that Jesus announces places him implicitly in tension with the Roman imperial leaders and their local affiliates: the Herodian rulers and the chief priests of Jerusalem. Luke explicitly identifies Caesar Augustus as the reigning ruler at Jesus' birth (2:1-2). Then, since the angels who announce Jesus' birth acclaim him as "Savior" and further elaborate that "peace" is the blessing now given from on high, Luke implicitly places Jesus' mission in tension with the claims of Augustus and the imperial order existing under him.

As his ministry progresses, Jesus provides various indications that his model of service and humility is profoundly in tension with what can be termed the "domination model" of the Romans and their allies. This distinction is prominent in the Lukan report of Jesus' final supper with his disciples. In his supper teaching Jesus expressly rejects the pattern of "the rulers of the Gentiles" who exercise "lordship" over their subjects and delight in receiving from them the honorific title of "Benefactor." It shall not be so for his disciples. Jesus tells them: "rather let the greatest among you become as the youngest, and the leader as one who serves" (22:26b).

As noted above, after describing the initial ministry in Galilee, Luke portrays Jesus making a momentous journey to Jerusalem that begins at 9:51 and does not end until 19:44. Just before he commences this decisive journey, Jesus indicates to his disciples that at its end he will suffer much from the chief priests and their allies and be killed, but on the third day he will be raised (9:22; see also 9:43). During the course of his journey Jesus briefly alludes to his coming suffering (17:25) and then, as he draws close to the city, he provides his third and most detailed prediction of what will occur (18:31-34). In this statement he predicts the involvement of the Gentiles (i.e., the Romans) in his death, expressly indicating their scourging and mocking of him. Significantly, Jesus again closes this prediction with a reference to his rising on the third day.

Once he reaches Jerusalem, Jesus' symbolic protest at the Temple and his parable concerning "wicked tenants" who will be expelled from the vineyard profoundly challenge the chief priests and their lay allies. A complex series of interactions and maneuvers then ensues (including Jesus' final interactions with his disciples), with the end result that the chief priests arrest Jesus and hand him over to Pilate on charges that he is stirring unrest and constituting a threat to Caesar's rule (23:2).

Both during the trial before Pilate and in the subsidiary hearing with Herod Antipas the chief priests are intractable in their opposition. Ultimately Pilate accedes to the priests' demand and orders Jesus' crucifixion. Jesus' demeanor before Pilate and Herod cannot be characterized as either deferential or obsequious. Even with death approaching, Jesus' responses to the women of Jerusalem (23:27-31) and the penitent thief on the cross (23:40-43) still display the characteristics of one who offers salvation. Yet in the events of his suffering and death his power to confer salvation has seemingly dissipated. This startling downward turn is now accentuated by the taunts and mockery he endures.

Jesus has taught and ministered as one truly a Savior, yet now he is subjected to abject humiliation and to death. The derisive taunts of the chief priests as he hangs on the cross focus on his failure as a purported savior: "He *saved others*; let him *save himself*" (23:35a; emphasis added). The crucifying soldiers likewise ridicule his saving mission: "If you are the king of the Jews, *save* yourself!" (23:37; emphasis added). The reproach of the unrepentant thief further highlights Jesus' seeming inability to save *anyone*: "Are you not the Christ? *Save yourself and us!*" (23:39; emphasis added).

Given Luke's emphasis on the power of the crucifixion to destroy Jesus' standing as Savior, it seems evident that Luke's narrative concerning Jesus' resurrection implicitly represents a decisive reaffirmation of Jesus as the bringer of salvation. This salvation has *not* been placed in jeopardy by the suffering and crucifixion of its bringer.

Indeed, at the close of his Gospel Luke emphasizes the *necessity* of the suffering and death Jesus endured. The angels at the tomb remind the women that Jesus himself had earlier indicated that he would suffer handing over and crucifixion (24:7). Jesus himself evidences this perspective in speaking with the two disciples on the Emmaus road (24:26). He then subsequently repeats and amplifies this necessity of suffering in his appearance to the apostles and other disciples gathered in the upper room later that evening (24:45-46).

3. The Disciples and Apostles of Jesus in Luke[3]

Luke records Peter's spoken words in eight scenes and portrays him speaking twice in one of these scenes (5:5, 8) and three times in another (22:57, 58b, 60). The significance and frequency of his spoken words (setting aside for the moment Peter's substantive role within the Gospel's plot) are themselves indicators of Peter's prominence in the Gospel. Nevertheless, Luke does not portray Peter as an isolated disciple of Jesus, but rather as a member of a larger group of disciples. It is thus appropriate to approach this evangelist's portrayal of Peter through an analysis focusing on the larger groups of disciples and apostles whom Jesus sovereignly calls.

A. *Jesus' Authority Over His Disciples*

The simple yet fundamental point to be focused on in this section is that Jesus is the one who authoritatively calls and teaches his first disciples. Further, he is the one who guides them throughout the journey they make together. Jesus' decisive call to Peter will be considered in the following subsection. Here it suffices to reference Jesus' utter seriousness and deliberateness in selecting his inner group of twelve disciples. According to Luke's report, Jesus took this step after extended, nightlong prayer:

> In these days he went out to the mountain to pray; and all night he continued in prayer to God. And when it was day, he called his disciples, and chose from them twelve, whom he named apostles. (6:12-13)

B. *The Mission of the Apostles and Disciples in Luke*

Luke does not begin the phase of Jesus' story that involves the calling and teaching of his disciples until chapter 5. As related above, Jesus' public ministry opens in the synagogue at Nazareth (4:16-30), but he gains no disciples at this event. Only later, after ministering briefly in neighboring Capernaum, does he gather his first disciples: Peter, James, and John.

In Luke's narrative Jesus enters Peter's house and heals his mother-in-law (4:38-39) before the lakeshore scene in which he formally calls Peter and Peter's partners, James and John (5:1-11). Levi is the next disciple called by name (5:27). That the total number of disciples grows well beyond the first five is indicated clearly when Luke subsequently reports that Jesus now possesses a larger group of disciples from whom he selects a subgroup numbering twelve (6:13a). Jesus now specifically names the twelve disciples who comprise this group "apostles" (6:13b). Luke underscores the significance of this initiative in two ways. First, as already observed, Luke portrays Jesus withdrawing to a mountain and spending the entire night in prayer before making this selection (6:12). Second, Luke then provides a complete list of those selected as apostles, supplying additional brief notes after the names of six of them (6:14-16).

These Twelve are closely associated with Jesus as he conducts his ministry in the cities and villages of Galilee: "And the twelve were with him" (8:1b). As discussed in section two above, Jesus' public ministry can be characterized in terms of "the bringing of salvation." In 9:1-6 and 9:10 Jesus enables the twelve apostles to have some participation in this mission. Luke reports that Jesus "gave them power and authority over all demons and to cure diseases." The apostles successfully carry out this mission, eventually reporting back to Jesus concerning their work of preaching and healing.

Jesus subsequently takes the apostles with him to Bethsaida where they (despite initial hesitation) assist him in the arrangements for the miraculous feeding of the five thousand. At the conclusion of this miracle (9:10-17) the fragments of the multiplied bread fill twelve baskets, a number that Luke's paradigmatic readers link to his later description of Jesus appointing his apostles as judges of the twelve tribes of Israel (22:28-30).

That Luke has in view a grouping of disciples that extends beyond the Twelve can also be established from his narrative. At 10:1 Jesus explicitly appoints seventy "others" to travel ahead of him, preparing for his arrival at the locations he intends to visit. These other disciples are given travel instructions that are largely comparable to those previously given to the Twelve (compare 10:3-12 with 9:1-5, noting that at 9:1 the Twelve are explicitly given "power and authority over all demons and to cure diseases."

As Luke's narrative unfolds there are four internal predictive prolepses in which Jesus predicts his rejection and/or death (9:22; 9:44; 17:25; 18:31-33). Addressed to all his disciples, Jesus' first prediction (9:22) comes right after Peter has confessed that Jesus is the Christ. Jesus then explains that his followers must themselves be prepared to take up the cross and lose their lives (9:23-26). Luke reports no response whatsoever by Peter, by the Twelve, or by any of the disciples to these startling and challenging words. Rather, the passage that follows immediately in the narrative concerns Jesus' transfiguration.

Jesus' second prediction that he will be delivered up to his enemies comes at 9:44 and is again addressed to the disciples as a group. Here Luke indicates that their response was a lack of comprehension of the meaning of Jesus' words. Luke also includes the exculpatory statement that they did not understand this saying because "it was concealed from them" (9:45). In the next scene of the Gospel Jesus himself deals with another failing by his disciples. Perceiving their competition regarding greatness and knowing the thoughts residing in their hearts, Jesus places a child at his side and instructs the disciples that true greatness comes from receiving persons with the humble standing of such a child (9:47-48).

In chapter 17, within his discourse to his disciples about being prepared for the final coming of the Son of Man (17:22-37), Jesus indicates that his own suffering and rejection must first occur (17:25). As with the previous two predictions, Luke reports no reaction by the disciples to this ominous statement. Later in the narrative Jesus takes the Twelve aside to share with them his final and most elaborate prediction of what is to occur when they reach Jerusalem (18:31-33). Once again Luke portrays a lack of comprehension regarding Jesus' shocking words. Here Luke's exculpatory comment is that "this saying was hid from them" (18:34b).

When Jesus gathers with the apostles for a final supper (22:14), Luke portrays him making a series of internal and external predictions. These predictions concern the apostles' behavior that night as well as Peter's future behavior. (See the treatment of 22:31-32 in the following section.) Jesus' first prediction concerns his betrayal by one of them (22:21-22). What is the response by the apostles to this prediction? Their first response is not to deny that such a betrayal will occur, but rather to address questions to one another (22:23). Then, in a scenario reminiscent of what occurred after Jesus had previously predicted his handing over (9:44), his selected apostles begin to dispute about their respective greatness (22:24)!

What estimation should be placed on the performance of Jesus' disciples, particularly his twelve apostles, at this juncture? Initially they accepted Jesus' call and shared with some success in his mission of bringing salvation. Nevertheless, when Jesus introduces the topic of his coming suffering and death, Luke presents their basic response as silence. They never expressly reject the scenario he predicts, but rather seem incapable of apprehending it, let alone embracing it. Even more negatively, in the immediate aftermath of Jesus' predictions of his coming travail Luke has twice portrayed them engaging in self-centered arguments concerning their own rank and greatness.

Still, despite their lack of appreciation for the suffering he will endure, and despite their failure to embrace humble service, Jesus continues to choose them! At 22:25-27 Jesus instructs them anew regarding service and humility, this time using the dominationist conduct of the Roman authorities as a negative example. He then expresses an assessment of his apostles that seemingly passes over their self-seeking. Referencing their perseverance in following him, Jesus expresses a promise ordered to a future that is almost beyond the apostles' horizon (external predictive prolepsis):

> You are those who have continued with me in my trials; and I assign to you, as my Father assigned to me, a kingdom, that you may eat and drink at my table in my kingdom, and sit on thrones judging the *twelve* tribes of Israel. (Luke 22:28-30; emphasis added)

Section three below will show that Jesus followed this general prediction regarding the Twelve with a complex prediction concerning Peter's role in thwarting Satan's purposes. For Satan has re-emerged to pose a serious challenge to Jesus' accomplishment of his mission. Both these predictions take on added dimensions of meaning when Luke's paradigmatic readers reflect that Jesus articulates them just before the scene of Jesus' disciples (Peter included) sleeping at Gethsemane and just before the scene of Peter's denials.

One other facet of Luke's narrative should not escape notice: the disappearance of the apostles from the story once Jesus is arrested. One of the disciples impulsively delivers a sword blow to a member of the arresting party, only to earn Jesus' rebuke and his intervention to heal the head wound (22:50-51). Apart from this Luke relates nothing regarding the response of the apostles to Jesus' arrest. As his narrative unfolds, Luke focuses on Peter's denials. Luke reports nothing more regarding the behavior or even the location of the other ten apostles until Jesus' appearances to them after his resurrection. They along with Peter are completely absent from scenes of his Roman trials and the crucifixion, unless Luke's references to "acquaintances" standing securely at a distance (23:49) can be taken to allow a minimal presence for members of the Twelve.

4. Peter during the Time of Jesus' Public Ministry[4]

A. *The Names of Peter*

Within the course of his narrative Luke mentions Simon/Peter thirty times.[5] In the first scenes of Jesus' public ministry Luke's preferred name for this disciple is "Simon." (The single exception to this usage is at 5:8 where Luke uses "Simon Peter.") At 6:14, in listing the twelve apostles, Luke lists Simon first and also indicates that Jesus changed Simon's name to "Peter." Luke here reports this change of name without indicating Jesus' rationale for making it. It will be seen below that Luke 22:32-34 sheds some light on the meaning Jesus intends by this new name. After 6:14 Luke consistently refers to this apostle as "Peter."[6]

B. *Luke's Portrayal of Peter Before the Last Supper*

Luke's first reference to Peter establishes that he has a house and implies that his mother-in-law lives with him (4:38). Whether Peter's wife is alive is not disclosed. Significantly, even before Jesus calls Peter into discipleship he enters Peter's house and heals Peter's mother-in-law from the high fever that was afflicting her (4:39). The call of Peter follows after these initial contacts. Jesus thus knows something about Peter before he dramatically summons him into discipleship.

Within 5:1-11 the two directives spoken by Jesus and the two responses given by Peter are of critical importance. However, before we proceed to an analysis of these four quotations it is initially useful to identify some of the other features Luke includes in his presentation of this scene.

First, there are two boats at the side of the lake. One of them belongs to Peter, and Jesus effectively commandeers it (5:2-3). Second, James and John are named as partners with Peter (5:7, 10) a feature that will become even more significant when Jesus subsequently selects them as apostles. Third, the catch of fish is immense (5:6-7). Fourth, the call Jesus explicitly addresses to Peter also invites the others fishing with him: At 5:11 Luke shows them joining in the same radical response to Jesus that Peter makes, leaving "all" to follow Jesus. Consider now the first exchange between Jesus and Peter. Jesus' words are directed to Simon even though the verb forms used indicate that others will be involved in carrying out his command:

Jesus: "Put out into the deep and let down your nets for a catch." (5:4)

Peter: "Master, *we* have toiled all night and taken nothing! But at your word *I* will let down the nets." (5:5; emphasis added)

Clearly, Jesus' directives are authoritatively given. There is no mistaking his intent. Peter's response is decisive compliance—there is no hesitation on his part. Given Luke's earlier presentation of Mary's full-hearted compliance with the angel Gabriel's annunciation, it is possible for paradigmatic readers to see Peter echoing Mary's obedience here. Notice that Peter's response indicates his personal willingness to trust Jesus' *word* just as Mary earlier expressed her personal willingness to trust the angel Gabriel's *word* (1:38b).

The second exchange occurs after Peter and his partners have experienced the astonishingly abundant, overflowing catch of fish. Now Peter initiates the exchange. Falling worshipfully at Jesus' knees, he implores:

> *Peter:* "Depart from *me*, O Lord, for *I* am a sinful man." (5:8b; emphasis added)
>
> *Jesus:* "Do not be afraid; henceforth *you* will be catching people." (5:10b, NSRV; emphasis added)

In this exchange the interaction between Jesus and Peter is highly personal. Peter addresses Jesus directly and with an intensity that is almost visceral. Falling to his knees, he confesses his sinfulness to Jesus, whom he addresses with great reverence as "Lord." He bids Jesus, his Lord, to depart from him. Such is Peter's recognition of his own sinfulness when faced with the majestic power of Jesus. Yet Jesus will not follow Peter's bidding to leave, for from its beginning to its end this scene discloses that Jesus has a particular mission in view for Simon. Indeed, Jesus virtually "overwhelms" this fisherman because of the more important calling he desires to bestow on him. Because he intends to recruit Simon, personally and directly, for the mission of "catching human beings," Jesus manifests an extraordinary display of his sovereign power. And he is not dissuaded from his purpose by Simon's protestations regarding his sinfulness.

In making this great catch of fish Peter did not act alone, but rather was assisted by others. Luke reports that all who were with him in the boat were as astonished as Peter at the great catch (5:9b). So also were James and John, Peter's partners in the other boat (5:10). At the very end of the scene Luke says that "they" brought their boats to land and then left everything and followed Jesus (5:11).

James and John, the sons of Zebedee, also become Jesus' disciples as a result of this event. Like Peter, they now leave everything to follow Jesus. Nevertheless, Peter plays the pivotal role in this scene. Peter is the one Jesus authoritatively directs to put out into the deep for a catch. He personally is the one to whom Jesus addresses the words "do not be afraid" (5:10b). And he personally is the one to whom Jesus addresses the decisive call to future mission:[7] "henceforth you will be catching people" (5:10c). Within Luke's narrative framework Peter's pivotal role in this scene anticipates the crucial role he will later play in strengthening the other apostles against Satan's sifting (22:31-32; see below).

Simon next appears in the scene in which Jesus designates him and eleven other disciples as apostles. Two details Luke includes here highlight the significance of the steps he shows Jesus taking. The solemn setting is that of a mountain. Further, Jesus prays the entire night to God. For Luke's paradigmatic readers these details connect this scene with the Transfiguration scene in Luke 9. In the latter scene Jesus will again ascend a mountain and he will again spend the night in prayer.[8] In the present scene he selects Simon and eleven others as his twelve apostles and invests Simon with a new name. In the second scene he selects Peter, James, and John from the other disciples and affords them the privilege and challenge of observing his transfiguration.

In addition to positioning him first on his list of apostles, Luke also adds to Simon's stature by including the report that Jesus gave him the name "Peter." At this time nothing in Luke's account explains Jesus' rationale for such a step. Nevertheless, when 6:13-14 (in which Simon is selected as the first apostle and given a new name) is read in the light of 5:1-11 (in which Simon is the first disciple called and commissioned as a fisher of human beings), the step of renaming seems to represent Jesus' further "honoring" of Simon even if the meaning of this new name is not immediately clear. (The initial impression of Luke's paradigmatic readers that the new name somehow honors Simon will be confirmed when they reach 22:31-34 and discern that the name "Peter" can be connected to Simon's role of strengthening the other apostles.)

Subsequently Jesus instructs his disciples, Peter presumably included, in his great Sermon on the Plain (6:20-46). Various disciples, including the Twelve, then travel with Jesus in his visits to the cities and villages of Galilee (8:1-3). Unnamed disciples then accompany him when he accomplishes various miraculous healings and travels by boat trip to the other side of the Sea of Galilee. They are similarly present to observe the two healings he accomplishes on his return.

As part of his description of Jesus' healing of the woman with the flow of blood, Luke relates a line spoken by Peter in an effort to reassure Jesus that no one has touched him purposefully (8:45b): "Master, the multitudes surround you and press upon you!" It is also significant that when Jesus arrives to restore the ruler's daughter he permits no one to enter the house with him *except* Peter, John, and James, along with the child's parents (8:51).

It is after this latter healing that Jesus formally entrusts power and authority to the group of apostles as he sends them out to preach the reign of God and to heal (9:1-6). Upon their return the apostles assist Jesus in a minor way when he effects the miraculous feeding of the five thousand (9:10-17). After this event, in response to Jesus' query, Peter expressly confesses Jesus' identity as the Christ.

To appreciate Luke's presentation of Peter's confession it should be recalled that at the birth of Jesus angels proclaimed to shepherds that the child born in Bethlehem is "Christ the Lord" (2:11). Also, when his parents later bring the child to the Temple in Jerusalem, Luke provides another vivid scene in which the aged Simeon comes forward to confirm that Jesus is indeed the Christ (2:25-35). Further, at 4:41b Luke shows Jesus rebuking the expelled demons and forbidding them to speak because they know that he is the Christ.

Within Luke's narrative, then, Peter is not the first human being to know that Jesus is the Christ (the shepherds and Simeon know), nor is he the first to proclaim this truth (Simeon has already done so). Nevertheless, Peter is the first to proclaim this during the course of Jesus' public ministry and Jesus' acknowledgment of Peter's confession signals that the way is open for his other disciples to ponder and accept this aspect of Jesus' identity. As the following excerpt from Luke's ninth chapter indicates, Jesus' response is first to mandate silence from all present. He then discloses that he will suffer, die, and rise, and challenges them to their own embrace of the cross and the possible loss of their lives for his sake. All of these facets are seen here:

> And he said to them, "But who do you say that I am?" And Peter answered, "The Messiah of God." He sternly ordered and commanded them not to tell anyone, saying, "The Son of Man must undergo great suffering, and be rejected by the elders, chief priests, and scribes, and be killed, and on the third day be raised." Then he said to them all, "If any want to become my followers, let them deny themselves and take up their cross daily and follow me. For those who want to save their life will lose it, and those who lose their life for my sake will save it. What does it profit them if they gain the whole world, but lose or forfeit themselves? (9:20-25, *NRSV*)

Luke portrays no response by Peter or any of the others present to these stunning words by Jesus. Jesus has predicted his suffering, rejection, and death and has challenged his hearers to embrace the cross daily, counseling that by losing their lives they will save them. Instead of recording any shock, questions, or disavowals by Peter and the others, Luke leaves Jesus' challenging words "suspended in the air," as it were. His narrative then proceeds directly to the major event of the Transfiguration (9:28-36).

Just as he earlier invited Peter, John, and James to accompany him inside the ruler's house, Jesus now selects Peter, John, and James to accompany him onto the mountain to pray. Luke reports that as the Transfiguration began to occur, "Peter and those with him were heavy with sleep" (9:32a). When the three apostles awaken, Peter takes the initiative, saying to Jesus, "Master, it is well that we are here; let us make three booths, one for you and one for Moses and one for Elijah" (9:33b). For Luke's paradigmatic readers this bold statement likely serves to enhance Peter's standing. However, Luke's subsequent narrator's comment at 9:33c, "not knowing what he said," tends to diminish the nobleness of the words Peter has just uttered.

Nevertheless, when Luke's transfiguration narrative is considered in all its components its fundamentally positive portrayal of Peter is unmistakable. Peter is the first named of the three Jesus selects to accompany him. Second, Peter's key response to the stunning vision is positive even though he hardly knows what to say. Third, after Peter speaks he and the two others are given the privilege of being enveloped miraculously by a cloud and hearing a voice from within the cloud state the majestic words, "This is my Son, my Chosen; listen to him" (9:35). In effect, then, Peter, John, and James have been selected to be present for a theophany, an awesome manifestation of God. Luke then concludes his report by indicating that after the vision ended and Jesus was alone the three apostles maintained a reverent silence about all they had been privileged to experience.

Luke has thus far in his narrative presented Peter in generally favorable terms. The same assessment may be given for the other apostles and disciples up to this point. It is only at 9:45-48 that Luke first imparts a negative perspective relative to Jesus' disciples. After Jesus' second Passion prediction Luke reports that the disciples did not understand Jesus' words and were afraid to ask him about them (9:44-45). Luke then includes a passage that portrays Jesus' followers quarrelling over greatness, although none of those so portrayed is identified by name. This argument over greatness does not result in a sharp rebuke; Jesus rather seeks to correct this behavior by his own example in welcoming a child to his side. To the degree that the disciples welcome the very least, they shall be regarded as great (9:46-48).

If the foregoing passage portrays Jesus' disciples experiencing difficulty in upholding his teaching on humility and service, one of the next passages in Luke's narrative indicates that at least two of the apostles have not grasped Jesus' challenging teaching against harming persons through violence. In 9:51-56 James and John receive Jesus' rebuke for proposing he call down fire to destroy a Samaritan village that has proved inhospitable to them. Peter is not included in this rebuke, yet the passage provides a further indication that the disciples as a whole are not grasping fundamental features in their master's approach.

As noted above, Luke structures the central section of his Gospel (9:51–19:40) around Jesus' extended journey to Jerusalem. There are two instances within this journey in which Luke portrays Peter stepping forward to ask that Jesus clarify a teaching he has just given. In the first instance (12:41) Peter simply asks directly, "Lord, are you telling this parable for us or for all?" The second occurs after Jesus' challenging response to the rich ruler about selling all his goods so as to distribute to the poor. Those standing near ask who can be saved, only to have Jesus reply that what is impossible for humans is possible for God (18:18-27). At this point Peter speaks out (18:28): "Lord, we have left our homes and followed you." Jesus' reply is highly affirmative for all who have left home or family for the sake of the reign of God (18:29-30).

As Jesus draws near to Jerusalem he shares this third and most extensive prediction of his Passion and resurrection with the Twelve (18:31-34). Peter obviously hears this prediction. Yet, as was explicitly the case after the second prediction, none of those receiving this prediction grasp its meaning; in Luke's own explanation, its meaning was hidden from them. To focus on Peter's performance in Luke it is important to note that, despite having shared a highly privileged experience with Jesus at the time of his call and again at the time of the Transfiguration, Peter at this time is still far from comprehending the path Jesus will follow.

C. *Peter from Last Supper to Crucifixion*

Because Luke features Peter in a complex series of developments at the time of the Passover Supper, it is appropriate to focus attention on these reports by treating them in a separate subsection. Within Luke's narrative Jesus has now entered Jerusalem and initiated a confrontation with the chief priests and their allies (in particular 19:45-47 and 20:9-18) with the result that they have now begun to implement a plan for his death (20:20; 22:2). At this juncture Luke reports Satan's re-emergence and his success in entering into Judas (22:3).

Judas' machinations with the chief priests are thus occurring in the background as Jesus selects Peter and John to make the necessary preparations for the meal, giving them detailed instruction about meeting a man who would lead them to a large upper room. In accordance with these instructions the two apostles then prepare the Passover (22:8-13).

From the beginning of the supper until its conclusion, Jesus' sovereignty and his desire to benefit his disciples are evident through several initiatives. Jesus' favorable stance toward the apostles even in the face of Judas' betrayal and Peter's denial, is noteworthy (22:15): "I have earnestly desired to eat this Passover with you before I suffer . . ." Jesus then announces solemnly that the bread and wine he now blesses are his body and blood given for them (22:17-20). However, as soon as he completes this momentous pronouncement Jesus indicates that one of those present will betray him (22:22). At first the apostles question among themselves as to the identity of the betrayer (22:23). Then, however, they all begin to carry out a form of betrayal by disputing over who is the greatest among them (22:24).

Jesus rebukes the apostles for such quarrelling and instructs them once again regarding service (22:25-27). Without apparent pause he then commends them for their perseverance and makes an astonishing promise to them that they will sit on thrones judging the twelve tribes of Israel (22:28-30). This promise has been alluded to in section three of this chapter. Jesus' next words regarding Satan's threat occur within the context of that promise:[9]

> "Simon, Simon, behold, Satan demanded to have *you* (plural) that he might sift *you* (plural) like wheat, but I have prayed for *you* (singular) that *your* (singular) faith may not fail; and when *you* (singular) have turned again, strengthen your brethren." And he said to him, "Lord, I am ready to go with you to prison and to death." He said, "I tell you, Peter, the cock will not crow this day until you three times deny that you know me." (22:31-34; emphasis added)

What does the present passage signal in reference to Jesus' intention to establish the apostles on thrones judging the twelve tribes of Israel? In effect Satan's intended siftings pose a serious threat to the achievement of Jesus' purpose. Satan desires to obstruct Jesus' intended outcome by sifting the apostles, i.e., Peter and the others, like wheat. Indeed, Satan has already made some gains in accomplishing this objective. Just minutes earlier, on this very evening, the disciples of Jesus have fallen into the trap of disputing over their respective rankings in terms of greatness and in the hours ahead Peter's own denials loom. It is crucial for the plot of Luke's Gospel that Jesus now respond to the threat posed by Satan.

Perhaps more than any other passage pertaining to Peter, the present one challenges Luke's paradigmatic readers to pay careful attention to its nuances.[10] There are subtleties of meaning in Jesus' ways of addressing Peter and describing his role. Also, the future Jesus predicts for Peter contains dimensions of internal prolepsis (Satan's sifting and Peter's turning) as well as external prolepsis (the continuation of Peter's ministry of strengthening). What is more, when this passage is re-read in light of Luke 24 it emerges that Peter's ministry of strengthening the ten and other disciples is not a phenomenon that will take place only after the Gospel narrative has ended. Rather, this prediction begins to be fulfilled in the events of Easter day itself.

At other places in Luke's Gospel in which he repeats the name of the addressee, Jesus' usage implies a degree of solicitude or compassion for the person or entity to whom he speaks ("Martha, Martha" at 10:41 and "Jerusalem, Jerusalem" at 13:34). Jesus' use of "Simon, Simon" in the present verse thus signals his solicitude for this disciple and is consistent with the step he now takes in terms of assigning an important new ministry to him.

However, just three verses later Jesus addresses this same disciple as "Peter," causing us to question the meaning Luke intends his paradigmatic readers to discern in Jesus' shift of names. Two aspects of Luke's overall presentation pertain to the present question: (a) Only in this passage does Jesus address this disciple by name. While he speaks directly to him at 5:4 and 5:10 and frequently responds to questions and comments presented by this disciple, only here does Jesus call him by his name(s); (b) At 6:14, when Luke provides the list of Jesus' twelve apostles, he positions Simon first and appends an explanatory clause, "whom he named Peter." The Greek meaning of "Peter" is "Rock." Nevertheless, neither in Luke 6 nor in any other part of the Gospel except for the present verse is there any intimation of Jesus' reason for wanting Simon to have the additional name of "Rock."

With its reference to Peter's role as a source of strength for his brethren, the present passage suggests Jesus' rationale. In effect, the important ministry Simon will have in strengthening his brethren is the explanation for the bestowal of the name "Peter." Having just intimated why such a name is appropriate, Jesus now uses this name for *the first and only time* in the Gospel.

Given the phenomenon of Peter's denials, there may also be a dimension of irony in Jesus' use of this name. In the events that will immediately unfold Peter will not be able to live up to his name: he will not be a "rock" when he denies Jesus three times.[11] Nevertheless, even though Peter's behavior in the next hours will be decidedly "unrocklike," Jesus still looks to a future in which Peter's renewed strength will enable him to be a source of strength for others.[12]

At this juncture it is useful to focus on the character of the disclosures Jesus now imparts to Peter. Now is the decisive time of sifting, and Jesus is personally intervening, by reason of his prayer, to safeguard the eleven remaining disciples from the "entering in" of Satan. This is indeed privileged knowledge. Earlier in the supper Jesus has disclosed that one of the Twelve would betray him. He now speaks confidentially with Peter, disclosing Satan's more ambitious "demand"[13] and indicating his own personal intervention.[14]

Jesus then indicates to Peter that his own specific "strategy" for responding to Satan's designs is to focus *on Peter*. Jesus' prayer will strengthen him so that his faith may not fail. Then it will be Peter's role, after he has "turned again," to strengthen his brethren. Clearly Jesus has elected to make Peter a pivotal figure in his own strategy for responding to Satan's challenge.[15]

Observe that Jesus' means for strengthening Peter is intercessory prayer. It is as though Luke's major spotlight is focused on Jesus, with Peter at another part of Luke's stage illumined by a lesser spotlight. Jesus is turned toward Peter. What is he doing? He is interceding for Peter through prayer—the only instance within the Gospel in which Jesus practices intercessory prayer for an individual.

At the same time that he is alerting Peter to the danger he faces and selecting him for an important role vis-à-vis the other disciples, Jesus is also fully aware that Peter will very shortly deny even knowing him. Jesus is thus able to respond immediately to Peter's boldly proclaimed willingness to go with Jesus "to prison and death." What is Peter's response to Jesus' devastating prediction of Peter's three denials? At this stage of Luke's narrative Peter's silence is deafening.

Within the overall plot development of Luke's Gospel, Jesus' prediction that Peter will have a pivotal role in strengthening the other apostles and disciples is highly significant. How will his prediction be fulfilled? Especially, how will it be fulfilled if Jesus' other prediction regarding Peter's denials is also fulfilled? In Luke's plot Jesus has formulated a strategy for coping with Satan's threat. Because Jesus has personally selected him, Peter has the crucial assignment of buttressing the other disciples. As the Gospel unfolds Peter does indeed carry out the strengthening ministry to which Jesus has sovereignly appointed him. Nevertheless, from this point forward Peter's trajectory traces out a series of steep declines and inclines.

Various events that now transpire can be grouped under the heading of Peter's sifting. Although Luke does not give the names of the disciples who fail to keep watch with Jesus at the Mount of Olives, surely Peter is implicitly among their number (22:45). Similarly, Peter must be reckoned as one of those present at the tumultuous scene in which Jesus is seized (22:47-53). Peter does then follow Jesus "at a distance." However, he soon denies Jesus three times, and in each instance Luke cites Peter's words of denial (22:54-60).

One further aspect of Peter's sifting arises from Luke's report that Jesus looks directly at Peter right after Peter voices his third denial (22:60b). There are two aspects of this report that deserve consideration. First, this eye contact underscores the personal breach of allegiance Peter has committed. As he meets Jesus' gaze, Peter's earlier profession, "I am ready to go with you to prison and to death," rings in his ears. Only hours earlier he had professed this personal allegiance to Jesus; now he has spoken three separate and distinct denials of any relationship with Jesus.

The second aspect is that Jesus' gaze marks the beginning of Peter's "turning." What is the first step in this process? It is that Peter exits and weeps bitterly (22:62). This remorse truly marks the beginning of Peter's turning, yet as Luke's narrative continues to unfold Peter is still subject to Satan's sifting. For despite his remorse Peter does not find the strength to be present either at Jesus' Roman trial or at his crucifixion.

Luke's paradigmatic readers may also note the absence of the other apostles from Jesus' trial and crucifixion. Satan has demanded to sift all of them and, for the time being, this sifting continues. Indeed, Luke's report of the steadfast presence at the cross and burial of the women who had followed Jesus from Galilee effectively underscores the absence of the apostles. The evangelist's note that "acquaintances" stood at a distance (23:49) is the only softening element in the drawing of a scene in which not one member of the Twelve is named as present.

5. Peter and the Risen Jesus

Jesus' prediction regarding the sifting that Peter and the other apostles would experience has now been partially fulfilled, and Jesus' prediction of Peter's "turning" has also been partially fulfilled (in his tears of repentance). After the Resurrection the faithful women who attended to Jesus' burial proceed to his tomb and, to their astonishment, encounter two angels who proclaim that Jesus has risen (24:1-7). Luke then indicates that the women hastened to announce the news to the apostles and the other disciples (24:9). The initial response of *the apostles* (specifically) is not to believe the women's testimony (24:11). The sifting of Jesus' apostles still continues!

The next stage of Peter's turning is now at hand.[16] Peter takes it upon himself to run to the tomb. While Luke does not portray him coming to belief at this time, the fact that Peter wonders to himself "at that which was come to pass" (24:12) is evidently a step forward from the initial disbelief he and the others had registered to the women.

In Luke's next scene the risen Jesus appears to two unnamed disciples who are traveling toward the village of Emmaus (24:13-33). During the course of their conversation with the unrecognized Jesus the two disciples relate the visit of the women to the tomb and supply this new information: "*Some* of those who were with us went to the tomb, and found it just as the women had said, but him they did not see" (24:24; emphasis added). Given Luke's report of Peter's visit to the tomb at 24:12, Peter is surely referenced within this "some." Luke may also be suggesting here that others followed Peter's lead.

Peter's complete turning is now shown to have been accomplished by the risen Jesus himself. From Luke's narrative it is not possible to ascertain the precise time (in relation to Jesus' appearance to the two disciples on the road to Emmaus) of Jesus' appearance to Peter. Given that Luke portrays the risen Jesus transcending the conventions of space and time, it is not possible to resolve this question. What may be said with certainty is that, according to Luke, Peter was the first disciple Jesus called (recall 5:1-10) and is now one of the first, or the first, to meet his risen Lord.

What the eleven (Peter included!) announce to the returning Emmaus travelers is that "The Lord has risen indeed and has appeared *to Simon*" (24:34; emphasis added). Not by any initiative of his own has Peter come back to full communion with his Lord. Rather, Peter's "return" to the fullness of discipleship has been accomplished by the sovereign initiative of his risen Lord.

In addition to indicating the completeness of Peter's turning, 24:34 also shows that Peter has now entered on his ministry of "strengthening" the other apostles.[17] Recall that Luke last mentioned the apostles at 24:11, when the women's testimony seemed to them to be "an idle tale." Now the ten other apostles join with Peter in proclaiming Jesus' resurrection to the two disciples from Emmaus (who already know it!). Who has galvanized them into making this proclamation? No one else than Peter! As a consequence of the risen Jesus' initiative in appearing to him, Peter has fully turned and the force of his testimony has been powerful enough to convince the other apostles to join in affirming Jesus' resurrection.

Luke's narrative next intimates that Peter's ministry of strengthening is not yet completed. For when Jesus appears to the entire assembled group some are "troubled" and have "questionings" in their hearts (24:38). Further, even after Jesus invites them to see his hands and feet and touch him, some still "disbelieved for joy and wondered" (24:41a). Nevertheless, Jesus continues to manifest his risen body to them and explains to them his fulfillment of the Scriptures, particularly those pertaining to the Christ's suffering. Further, he stresses to them "that repentance and forgiveness of sins should be preached in his name to all nations . . ." (24:47a). These words reference a future ministry that these disciples, Peter certainly included, will engage in.

Finally Jesus appoints all of them, Peter included but not specifically named, as "witnesses of these things" (24:48). This witnessing extends beyond the end of Luke's narrative and constitutes, along with Jesus' promise of the Spirit (24:49), the final instance of external predictive prolepsis within the Gospel. In the penultimate scene of the Gospel Jesus leads this group to Bethany, where he solemnly blesses them and parts from them (24:50-51). The Gospel then closes as the disciples return to Jerusalem and the Temple with great joy to continue in their blessing of God.

6. Summary of Luke's Portrayal of Peter

In five episodes stretching from Peter's first contact with Jesus to the Transfiguration Luke portrays Peter in distinctly favorable terms. After the Transfiguration Peter is presumably among those unnamed disciples who quarrel over greatness. Nevertheless, Peter continues to follow Jesus faithfully even though there are additional episodes in which he, along with the other disciples, fails to grasp Jesus' teachings. At the Last Supper, Luke portrays Peter even more auspiciously than in his portrayal at the time of Peter's confession of Jesus as the Christ. In this momentous setting Jesus assigns Peter a role in judging the twelve tribes of Israel. Peter will also have a personal role in "strengthening the brethren."

Just as Jesus has envisioned, Peter's denials ensue. However, the apprehended Jesus gazes on Peter and effectively starts him on the path to restoration. On the day of resurrection Peter encounters his risen Lord and then begins to strengthen the others by means of his own testimony. As a member of the assembled group Peter then receives Jesus' mandate for preaching repentance and the forgiveness of sins to all.

Summary of Peter's Trajectory and Predicted Future in Luke

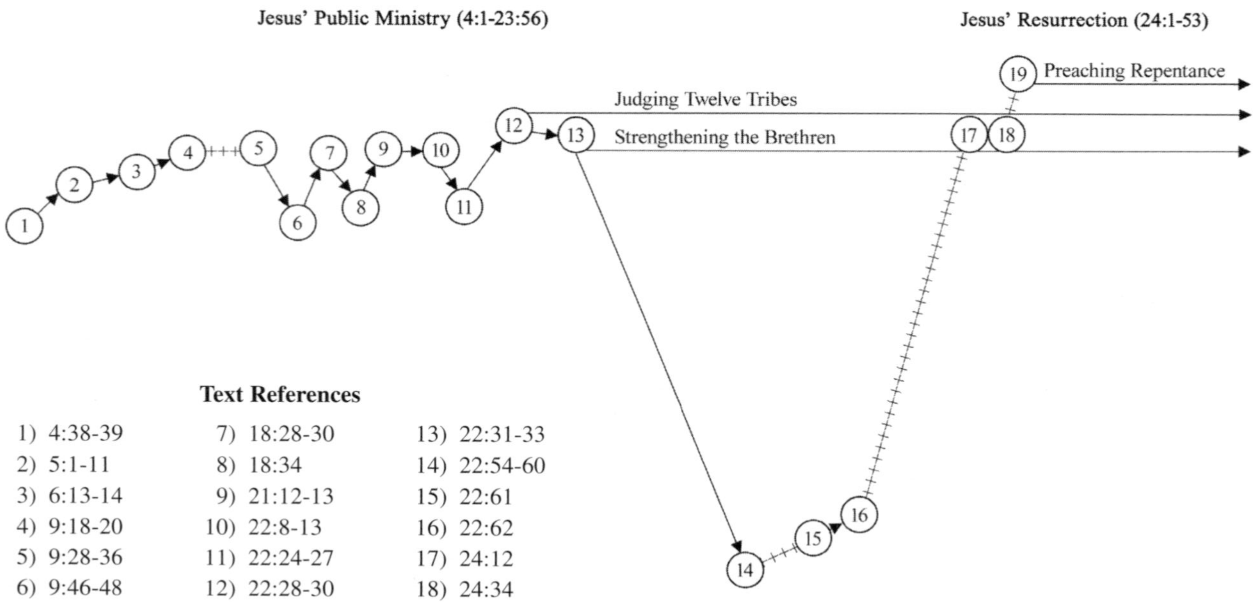

Text References

1) 4:38-39	7) 18:28-30	13) 22:31-33
2) 5:1-11	8) 18:34	14) 22:54-60
3) 6:13-14	9) 21:12-13	15) 22:61
4) 9:18-20	10) 22:8-13	16) 22:62
5) 9:28-36	11) 22:24-27	17) 24:12
6) 9:46-48	12) 22:28-30	18) 24:34
		19) 24:47

+ + + + Emphasizes Jesus' Sovereign Intervention

CHAPTER FOUR

Peter in Matthew's Gospel: The Name's the Thing by Which We Learn the Intentions of the King

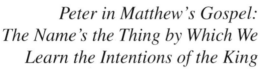

The first section of this chapter will briefly establish that Matthew's Gospel projects a future for Jesus' disciples, including Peter, that extends beyond the Gospel's final scene. The second section will then analyze Matthew's overall presentation of Jesus and his mission. Section three will take up the general portrayal of Jesus' disciples, and an extended analysis of the portrayal of Peter in Matthew's Gospel will be the topic of sections four and five.

1. The Future-Oriented Character of Matthew's Gospel

In analyzing the overall portrayal of Peter that Matthew provides in his Gospel it is important to observe at the outset that the final scene of this Gospel vividly looks to the future and contains a particularly rich instance of external predictive prolepsis. While Peter is not explicitly named in this scene, he is implicitly included in the future ministry Jesus here identifies for all of the eleven.

> Now the eleven disciples went to Galilee, to the mountain to which Jesus had directed them. And when they saw him they worshiped him; but some doubted. And Jesus came and said to them, "All authority in heaven and on earth has been given to me. Go therefore and make disciples of all nations, baptizing them in the name of the Father and of the Son and of the Holy Spirit, teaching them to observe all that I have

commanded you; and lo, I am with you to the close of the age." (28:16-20)

2. Jesus and his Mission According to Matthew

It is well known that Matthew shows Jesus delivering five major addresses or sermons. Each ends with a nearly identical Greek clause, and the conclusion of the final sermon includes the word "all" within it to indicate that Jesus has now completed all his major addresses. Perhaps because one of his own interests was to provide his readership with material that would be highly useful for catechesis, Matthew periodically halts his narrative to present these five major sermons.

Nevertheless, if we focus on another clause employed by Matthew it becomes clear that he is concerned with presenting Jesus' overall story in three parts.[1] This clause is "From that time Jesus began . . ." and Matthew uses it at 4:17 and 16:21. At 4:17 Matthew writes: "*From that time Jesus began* [to preach] . . ." and at 16:21 he employs the same formula with a variation: "*From that time Jesus began* [to show his disciples]. . . ."

Matthew's use of this formula thus segments the Gospel into three distinct parts: Part I, from 1:1 to 4:16; Part II, from 4:17 to 16:20; Part III, from 16:21 to 28:20. It is at 16:21, just after Peter has identified him as the Christ and Jesus has indicated that he will build a "church," that Matthew portrays Jesus decisively announcing that suffering, death, and resurrection lie ahead for him in Jerusalem.

In broad terms, Matthew uses the first section of the Gospel to introduce Jesus to his readership. This section includes Jesus' genealogy (1:1-17), an account of the circumstances of his birth (1:18-25), and an account of his baptism and temptation (3:13–4:11). Much more will be said below concerning Matthew's second section, but in general this section describes the principal features of Jesus' public ministry within Israel, including his stance toward the Jewish Law and other topics pertaining to ethics, his controversy with the Pharisees, and his initiative to establish a church. Some of these features continue to be present in section three. However, in this section Matthew's principal focus is on Jesus' turn toward his Passion and resurrection. Here he highlights Jesus' challenge to the chief priests in Jerusalem, his death at their instigation, and then, decisively, his resurrection.

It should be emphasized that well before Jesus begins his public ministry Matthew has indicated that Jesus has come within the context of an elaborately structured divine plan. Two references in Part I of the Gospel clearly establish this point. At 1:20 an angel tells Joseph that the child Mary has conceived is from the Holy Spirit. At 3:17, in the aftermath of Jesus' baptism, a voice from heaven announces: "This is my beloved Son, with whom I am well pleased." Thus when Jesus does begin to preach it is not surprising that he proclaims with assurance (4:17b): "Repent, for the kingdom of heaven is at hand."

This same quality of authoritativeness permeates the other two broad areas Matthew identifies for Jesus early in his ministry: healing and teaching. Matthew has a fondness for organizational patterns. We have already noted that (probably with the five books of Moses' Pentateuch in view) Matthew shows Jesus presenting his own teaching in five sermons. Another of Matthew's organizational techniques is evident in the Gospel's twelve references to Jesus' fulfillment of the Jewish prophets. In two cases Jesus himself asserts that he is fulfilling what was prophesied, and in ten other instances Matthew, as narrator, tells his readers that a given step or event in Jesus' ministry occurred in order that a prophecy might be fulfilled.

In Matthew's presentation, Jesus *alone* has the capacity to interpret the Jewish Law adequately. In some cases Jesus counsels the fulfillment of the precepts of the Law. In other cases he takes the existing laws to a deeper level of obligation. In still other cases he sets aside what the Law mandates.

As Matthew's narrative unfolds, this quality of sovereignty regarding the interpretation of the Jewish Law brings Jesus into sharp controversy with the Pharisees. Matthew portrays Jesus' conflict with these opponents in memorably harsh terms. For example, it is at Matt 23:1-33 that Jesus speaks seven searing "woes" against the Pharisees as a group.

Particularly in the Sermon on the Mount, Matthew's Jesus teaches authoritatively regarding righteous conduct. It is fair to say that when the Gospel is read in its entirety Jesus clearly regards the Pharisees, and even more the chief priests, as unrighteous in their conduct. Significantly, during the course of the Sermon on the Mount, Jesus proclaims an exalted ethic of love of enemies (5:43-48). When he later finds himself surrounded by an arresting party orchestrated by his principal enemies, the chief priests, he himself practices this very teaching. With full composure he authoritatively forbids his disciples to use their swords on his behalf, admonishing (26:52): "Put your sword back into its place, for all who take the sword will perish by the sword."

If Jesus is authoritative in his interpretation of the Jewish Law and in his critique of the Pharisees, he is no less so in denouncing the chief priests as corrupt and evil once he arrives in Jerusalem. Entering into the priest-controlled Temple, he drives out all who bought and sold and overturns the money-changing tables, decisively announcing that those responsible had made the Temple into a "den of robbers" (21:13b). Subsequently, before departing the Temple precincts for Bethany, Jesus delivers a further rebuke to the chief priests and scribes for their indignation over the hosannas now being offered Jesus (21:15-16).

The next day Jesus adroitly overcomes the challenge to his authority that the chief priests and elders present by posing to them a counter-question regarding the nature of John's baptism (21:23-27). Then, taking the offensive, he relates the parable of the two sons (21:28-32) with its insinuation that they, like the second son of the parable, were not doing the Father's will and were unrepentant about their lack of compliance. In even more incendiary fashion he then proceeds to tell publicly a parable about murderous, usurping, wicked tenants who were soon to be ejected from their positions and put to death by the owner to whom the vineyard truly belongs (21:33-41).

Matthew now depicts further maneuvering by the chief priests and the Pharisees working in alliance with them. Nevertheless, Jesus remains untouched by the maneuvers of his opponents and continues to teach publicly in the Temple, delivering at this point the blistering series of seven woes against the Pharisees referred to above.

As Passover now draws near, the chief priests begin to plot seriously how to destroy Jesus (26:3-5). Judas' defection to them from Jesus' inner circle (26:14-16) provides the linchpin securing their plot. Once they have taken Jesus into custody the chief priests and their allies relentlessly prosecute their case against him. When Pilate hesitates and then tries to distance himself from the verdict he will ultimately pronounce, the crowd, orchestrated by the chief priests, cries out that Pilate should let Jesus' blood be upon them (27:25). In effect, the chief priests and those under their influence emphatically assure Pilate that *they* (principally the chief priests) accept "responsibility" for any possible negatives arising out of Jesus' death. This figleaf having been tendered to him, Pilate, the Roman governor of Judea, then proceeds with Jesus' Roman crucifixion.

It is useful to summarize the aspects of Jesus' public ministry that have been identified to this point. They are: authoritative preaching, miraculous healings and other miracles, and authoritative teaching that initially engenders controversy with the Pharisees and then lethal controversy with the chief priests and their allies. One further aspect of Jesus' ministry according to Matthew now needs to be considered: his initiative in establishing a "church."

To appreciate this aspect of Jesus' endeavor, reference must be made to the Greek word *ekklēsia*, a word whose basic Greek meaning is "assembly." This word is commonly rendered into English as "church." Without providing a precise explanation of how this new assembly is to be understood,

Jesus in Matt 16:18 decisively announces that it is his intention to establish such a church.

In terms of the structure Matthew has given to his Gospel, the passage in which Jesus announces his intention to establish a church occupies a position of high prominence.[2] In response to Jesus' identity question Peter dramatically identifies him as "the Christ, the Son of the living God" (16:16). Jesus then responds to this confession by declaring with full sovereignty that Peter is blessed and Jesus intends to use him as the foundation rock for the church he will establish:

> And Jesus answered him, "Blessed are you, Simon Bar-Jona! For flesh and blood has not revealed this to *you*, but my Father who is in heaven. And I tell you, you are Peter, and on this rock *I will build my church*, and the powers of death shall not prevail against it. I will give you the keys of the kingdom of heaven, and whatever you bind on earth shall be bound in heaven, and whatever you loose on earth shall be loosed in heaven. Then he strictly charged the disciples to tell no one that he was the Christ." (Matt 16:17-20, author's translation; emphasis added)

Recall that in the next verse of his account (16:21) Matthew employs his trademark clause: "From that time Jesus began. . . ." This clause announces that a new section now begins, one in which the focus will be on Jesus' Passion and resurrection. However, in employing this clause Matthew simultaneously brings Part II of the Gospel to a close. The scene in which Jesus announces his intention of establishing a church, in effect, becomes the scene Matthew uses to end a major stage in Jesus' public ministry. Viewed from the standpoint of narrative structure, is Matthew not signaling to his paradigmatic readers that the founding of his church should be regarded as the culminating event in Jesus' public ministry prior to the turn toward suffering and death?

In a careful interpretation of 16:18-19 attention should also be paid to the significance of the first person singular pronouns (and one possessive adjective). Clearly, Jesus' use of "I" and "my" attest to the highly personal quality of the initiative he is undertaking. Jesus himself is initiating something new. He is the one who *will build* this new entity. And this church will belong *to him*.

Previously in his narrative Matthew has not portrayed Jesus as intending to establish a church. Jesus' selection of twelve apostles and his instructions to them (see the analysis of 10:1-42 below) may constitute a foreshadowing of a community entrusted with a mission. Nevertheless, the church Jesus now dramatically announces to Peter and the other disciples must be considered a bold new initiative that is scarcely anticipated in the previous events of Jesus' public ministry.

As previously noted, Jesus' Passion and resurrection emerge as the principal focus in Part III of Matthew's Gospel. Nevertheless, within Part III Jesus does provide several additional references to his church. These references occur within what is commonly referred to as "The Sermon on Church Life and Order" in Matthew 18. Jesus' words in this sermon presume that his church is a present reality. Second, by using the plural form of "you" Jesus now indicates that all of the church's members (not just Peter) participate in "binding and loosing." Further, Jesus affirms his own presence when two or three members of the church are gathered. These perspectives are present in the verses now to be cited and flow from Jesus' previous instructions (18:15-16) on correction of a brother or sister who is sinning:

> If he or she refuses to listen to them, tell it to the church; and if he or she refuses to listen even to the church, let him or her be to *you* as a Gentile and a tax collector. Truly, I say to *you*, whatever *you* bind on earth shall be loosed in heaven. Again I say to *you*, if two of *you* agree on earth about anything they ask, it will be done for them by my Father in heaven. For where two or three are gathered in my name, there am I in the midst of them. (Matt 18:17-20, author's translation; italics added to indicate plural form of "you")

Specifically, the two references to "the church" in this passage both pertain to the power of binding and loosing. The sinner reluctant to recognize his or her sin needs to be told by the church that the conduct in question is indeed a violation of Jesus' teaching. That the church, *as a community*, is authorized to perform this task is expressly indicated by Jesus' use of the plural in his words concerning binding and loosing in verses 18-19 in the above passage. All of "you," all the disciples as a group, now receive Jesus' authority for binding and loosing. Previously, in 16:19, this ministry was entrusted to Peter alone; now it is a ministry shared by the members of the church.

The importance of verses 19-20 should also not escape notice. Verse 19 carries forward the premise that conscientious endeavors by members of the church on earth (now the quorum is only two members!) will receive confirmation in the heavenly realm. Here the specific activity is prayer. If there is symphonious prayer on any topic by two members of the church, their prayer will be granted by Jesus' Father.

In verse 20 a further reality is said to characterize the assembly of two (or three) members of Jesus' church. Gathering in his name, they will find

Jesus himself present in their midst. This powerful reality of Jesus' presence in his church has already been foreshadowed by Matthew's reference at 1:23 of his infancy narrative. It is a reality that will be attested to by the risen Jesus at 28:20, the very last verse of the Gospel.

3. The Disciples of Jesus in Matthew[3]

Before we analyze Jesus' interactions with his disciples as a group it is useful to indicate how frequently Jesus and Peter communicate within Matthew's narrative. Peter speaks to Jesus in eleven scenes, speaking twice in three scenes and three times in one. In these scenes (also including 26:40) Jesus speaks explicitly to Peter a total of nine times.[4]

A. *Jesus' Sovereignty in Calling Disciples*

As noted, Jesus is highly authoritative as he teaches, heals, and preaches within Matthew's Gospel. This authoritativeness is also evident in the calling of the first disciples. Jesus is fully decisive when he approaches Peter and Andrew, and subsequently James and John. His sovereign invitation to both sets of brothers is: "Follow me." For their part, the response of these four to Jesus' initiative is also decisive. Trusting greatly in Jesus' call to become "fishers of human beings," they immediately leave everything to follow him (4:18-22).

B. *The Disciples and the Twelve*

These four disciples eventually constitute the nucleus of the Twelve.[5] Matthew indicates that Jesus subsequently gained other disciples and that Jesus called this larger group (including the two sets of brothers) to a "higher righteousness" as he instructed them in the Sermon on the Mount.

Matthew's Jesus expects his disciples to have a substantial faith. He underscores the importance of such faith at 8:23-27 when he sharply criticizes the unnamed disciples who are with him in the storm-tossed boat for being persons "of little faith." (He also uses this epithet at 6:30, 14:31, and 16:8.) Jesus then travels with a group of disciples during a preaching and healing ministry that extends to the time of the Mission Sermon in Matthew 10. It is during this interval, at 9:9, that Jesus decisively calls Matthew, the tax collector, as his fifth named disciple.

At the time of the Missionary Sermon seven additional disciples are named and, along with the five already identified, constitute the Twelve.

Peter heads this list, a prominence Matthew underscores with his use of the adjective "first." At 10:2 Matthew also describes these twelve as "apostles," the only time this term appears in his Gospel.

Within the twenty-eight chapters of Matthew there are only seven substantive references to the Twelve as a distinct group; four of these seven references occur at this point in the mission to Israel. One consequence of this pattern is that Peter is not characteristically portrayed as a significant figure among a well-defined group of twelve. Rather, his initiatives cause him to stand out from among a larger group simply described as "the disciples." Matthew's frequent references to unspecified groups of disciples have repercussions for the ministry of binding and loosing that is conferred by Jesus in chapter 18. This ministry, a complement to the ministry conferred on Peter in chapter 16, is now given by Jesus to all who comprise his church.

C. *The Performance of the Disciples in Part II of the Gospel*

Although the narrative does not indicate their success explicitly, Matthew's implied sense is that the Twelve faithfully carry forward the mission of preaching and healing (but not teaching) that Jesus entrusts to them at the beginning of chapter 10. Over the next chapters of the Gospel Jesus himself continues his own ministry to Israel, experiencing both acceptance and resistance. At this point Matthew's narrative is moving toward the high point of Peter's personal confession of Jesus at Caesarea Philippi and Jesus' declaration that he will establish a church. Yet before Matthew presents that culminating scene he narrates one other event pertaining to Jesus' identity, the storm on the lake, featuring a larger grouping of Jesus' disciples, with Peter included in the group.

Because of its significant contribution to Matthew's overall portrayal of Peter, a consideration of Peter's performance at 14:28-31 (when Jesus walks with him on the water) will be deferred until the following section of this chapter. Here the focus is on the response of the disciples who have been traveling in the boat with Peter. Pursuant to Jesus' instructions, this group of unnamed disciples has departed by boat to the other side of the lake. Jesus, much later in the night, comes toward them walking on the sea. The entire group of disciples is terrified and cries out in fear. In response, Jesus identifies himself to them and bids them not to fear.

It is at this juncture that Peter responds to Jesus with great boldness—but unsuccessfully! After Jesus rescues Peter, he and Peter get into the boat and the wind ceases. It is in their response to all of this that Jesus' disciples reach their highest level of performance. Note that Peter is implicitly included in this achievement since he is now again in the boat with the others.

As a group these disciples express the deepest understanding for Jesus that has heretofore been expressed in the Gospel. In Matthew's portrayal they now respond as follows:[6] "And those in the boat worshiped him, saying, 'Truly you are the son of God'" (14:33).

As Matthew's narrative proceeds, the disciples' standing diminishes slightly from the high point just reached. At 15:33 they once again do not grasp how the crowd of four thousand will be fed. More significantly, at 16:8 they earn Jesus' rebuke for being "of little faith" when they fail to grasp his warning about the leaven of the Pharisees and the Sadducees. Nevertheless, as Part II of the narrative concludes, the disciples and Peter especially are again cast in a favorable light as a consequence of their efforts to speak names that reflect Jesus' greatness (16:14-16). Matthew presumably portrays Jesus' esteem for his disciples, and Peter especially.

At 16:16, when Peter affirms Jesus' identity as "the Christ, the Son of the living God," Jesus' own response to Peter's confession is to pronounce a blessing on him and then to indicate the significant role and accompanying name he will have as a "rock" for Jesus' church. Matthew does not *explicitly* characterize the response of Peter or of any of the other disciples to these words. Yet is there not an implied sense that the disciples hardly know how to assess the project Jesus has just disclosed? Jesus closes this scene with an admonition to silence. The particular truth about which the disciples are to maintain silence is Jesus' identity as the Christ; no silence is explicitly mandated about the other principal topic of this scene: Jesus' intention to establish a church with Peter as its rock foundation.

D. *The Performance of the Disciples in Part III of the Gospel*

As noted above, Part II began with the scene in which Peter and Andrew were first called to be fishers for human beings. Now Matthew's trademark words at the beginning of 16:21, "From that time Jesus began to show his disciples" indicate that the third and final section of his Gospel is beginning. This section is dominated by the Passion and resurrection of Jesus, something Matthew signals explicitly in the second clause of 16:21 when Jesus declares "that he must go to Jerusalem and suffer many things from the elders and chief priests and scribes, and be killed, and on the third day be raised."

These words are, in fact, the first of three major prophecies concerning his Passion and resurrection that Jesus makes in this part of the Gospel. The other two predictions (17:22-23 and 20:18-19) will be treated below. It should also be noted that there are two other predictions focused on the Passion (apart from the Resurrection) at 17:12 and 26:2. All of these fall into the category of *internal* predictive prolepses.

Peter's agitated response to Jesus' first prophecy of his suffering and death is highly significant and will be analyzed in section four. At present the focus is on the explanatory reflections Jesus shares with the disciples as a group after he has sternly rebuked Peter. For Jesus now advises his disciples regarding two new startling and challenging requirements for discipleship: to deny their very selves and to take up their own crosses (16:24-26).

Matthew does not report any immediate negative response by the disciples to these new requirements. They all continue to journey forward with Jesus, especially Peter, James, and John, who experience the power of the Transfiguration (17:1-8). However, at 17:20 Jesus identifies the "little faith" of his disciples as the reason for their inability to exorcise a possessing spirit. Then, at 17:22-23, Matthew reports that the disciples were "greatly distressed" in hearing Jesus' second formal prediction of his Passion and resurrection. Subsequently Jesus' teaching that possessions constitute an impediment to the reign of God is profoundly disturbing to them (19:16-25). Nevertheless, in response to Peter's comment that the disciples have left all things to follow him (19:27), Jesus speaks words that are profoundly encouraging.

Significantly, the first part of Jesus' reply clearly focuses on the Twelve as a distinct group. Because they are a prediction of the standing the Twelve will have as a group at a time subsequent to Jesus' resurrection, these words represent an external predictive prolepsis:

> Jesus said to them, "Truly, I say to you, in the age to come, when the Son of Man shall sit on his glorious throne, you who have followed me will also sit on twelve thrones, judging the twelve tribes of Israel." (19:28, author's translation)

Jesus' words in this verse and his saying regarding eternal life in the immediately following verse (19:29) are clearly intended to encourage his disciples in their present path of discipleship. Nevertheless, as Matthew's narrative unfolds it becomes apparent that *present-day* glory as opposed to blessedness in the age to come is very much the preoccupation of at least James, John, and their mother. The self-seeking of these three[7] at 20:20-23 (and perhaps the implication is that the other ten also harbor such desires) is all the more egregious because Jesus has just pronounced the third prediction of his Passion and resurrection at 20:18-19.

Jesus responds to the indignation of the other ten toward James and John by providing an extended exposition regarding the path of service to which he is calling all of them (20:24-28). His followers are not to be influenced by the patterns of domination manifested by the Gentile rulers. Rather, they are to emulate the stance of the Son of Man who "came not to be served but to serve, and to give his life as a ransom for many" (20:28).

The disciples, including Peter and the Twelve, continue with Jesus into Jerusalem and implicitly remain present as Jesus engages in a series of challenges to the chief priests and their allies as well as a series of disputes with the Pharisees. In proximity to the Jerusalem Temple, Jesus proclaims his fifth sermon in the Gospel, the so-called "Apocalyptic Discourse" of 24:3–26:1. Included within this sermon are words alerting the disciples that tribulation and martyrdom lie ahead for them. Jesus' words at 24:9 thus constitute an external predictive analepsis pertaining to all the disciples, Peter certainly included: "Then they will deliver you up to tribulation, and put you to death; and you will be hated by all nations for my name's sake."

Subsequently Jesus gathers with the Twelve at the Last Supper, disclosing to them that one of them will betray him (26:20-21). After solemnly sharing bread and wine with them, Jesus then momentously predicts that all of them will fall away from him (26:31). He then adds this prediction and promise: "But after I am raised up, I will go before you to Galilee" (26:32).[8] This sequence of lapidary statements continues when Peter replies: "Though they all fall away because of you, I will never fall away" (26:33).

Jesus' own decisive reply to Peter's declaration is to aver that Peter will in fact deny him three times that very night. Rejecting Jesus' words, Peter makes a ringing proclamation of allegiance and Matthew reports that all the other ten joined in Peter's profession of undying fidelity. Because these words represent the highest standard that Peter and the other disciples ever attain to, it is important to cite Matthew's report in full: "Peter said to him, 'Even if I must die with you, I will not deny you.' And so said all the disciples" (26:35).

In the actual unfolding of events the twelve disciples cannot stand by their profession. Matthew relates at 26:56b: "Then all of the disciples forsook him and fled." And Peter, of course, soon proceeds to deny Jesus three times, just as predicted (26:69-75). So ends Matthew's pre-resurrection portrayal of the Twelve and Jesus' other disciples, save for the faithful women who follow Jesus to the cross and look on from afar (23:55-56). Matthew reports that Mary Magdalene "and the other Mary" even followed to the site of Jesus' burial (27:61) and also details the bold initiative of Joseph of Arimathea in providing for Jesus' entombment (27:57-60).

4. Peter During the Time of Jesus' Public Ministry[9]

Because Peter appears in several major and numerous minor ways within the Gospel, and because he is frequently portrayed in scenes that include the Twelve and others of Jesus' disciples, there is some difficulty in avoiding passages already treated in attempting to identify the various features of Matthew's overall portrayal of Peter. This section will have three components: a treatment of the name "Peter" and then an analysis of this disciple's role in Part II and Part III of the Gospel.

A. *The Names of Peter*

Matthew mentions Simon/Peter twenty-five times.[10] At the time of his calling Peter's name was Simon, but Jesus only addresses him as "Simon" in one place in the Gospel: at 17:25, where Jesus is not satisfied with Peter's answer to the collectors of the half-shekel tax.

At 4:18 Matthew narrates that Jesus invited "Simon *who is called Peter*" to become a fisher for human beings. Similarly at 10:2, in listing Jesus' twelve apostles, Matthew begins as follows: "first Simon *who is called Peter*." Throughout the Gospel Matthew consistently uses the name Peter in referring to this disciple, but it is not until 16:18 that he discloses the circumstances under which "Peter" became Simon's designated name.

In effect this pattern of usage serves to emphasize, especially for Matthew's paradigmatic readers, the importance Matthew attaches to Jesus' changing of Peter's name. The repetition of the clause "who is called Peter" at 4:18 and 10:2 encourages such questions as: (1) who is responsible for the fact that Simon is now called Peter? and (2) by what rationale does Simon appropriately have this new name?

In Matthew 16:17-18 the evangelist provides his readers with answers to both these questions. Recall that at the beginning of this series of interactions at 16:13-16 Peter has momentously affirmed that Jesus is the Christ. Next, in 16:17, Jesus cordially affirms that Simon has been blessed by Jesus' Father. Then, in 16:18, Jesus renames him as "Peter" and indicates that he will serve as the rock foundation for the church Jesus will build. Verse 19, in which Jesus entrusts Peter with the keys of the kingdom of heaven and the ministry of binding and loosing, closes this entire sequence.

In Matthew's careful rendering of the plot of the Gospel, Jesus' initiative in changing Simon's name is thus a central facet in a carefully presented sequence. First, Jesus is extremely pleased by Peter's confession and responds with a gracious beatitude to the Father for having prompted Peter to this insight. Jesus employs Peter's full name, "Simon bar-Jona" (literally Simon, son of Jonah) in this beatitude, a step that focuses even more attention on the fact that Jesus is about to take the sovereign step of renaming him.

Second, as an aspect of the plot of the Gospel, Jesus now discloses that he intends the building of a church. Third, it is because of Jesus' intention to build a church and because of the role he intends for Simon to fulfill within this church that Simon "requires" a new name.

What name shall Simon now have? Again, within Matthew's perspective Jesus does not rename Simon merely as a way of indicating a particular bond with him or as a means of honoring him. Rather, the new name that Jesus bestows has to do, fundamentally and logically, with a new role he is inviting Simon to fulfill.

What is the new role? As indicated previously, it is to be a rock foundation for Jesus' church. Because he is being given a new role, Simon shall have a new name that befits his role. His name will thus be "Peter" because that is his new role: to serve as a "Rock" for Jesus' church. Note that three sovereign initiatives are described in Matthew's portrayal here. With full sovereignty Jesus indicates that he intends to build a church. With full sovereignty Jesus selects Simon for an important new role as the rock foundation for his church. With full sovereignty and with strategic logic Jesus indicates that the disciple named "Simon" at birth shall henceforward be known as "Peter."

B. *Peter's General Portrayal in Part II of Matthew*

It is important to recognize that both in Part II and in Part III of his Gospel Matthew repeatedly uses a significant secondary spotlight to illuminate Peter for his audience. Within Part II of the Gospel Matthew's secondary spotlight falls on Peter in a total of six scenes. Peter is prominent in the first and last scene of this part of the Gospel and he is also prominent in 14:25-33, the scene in which he hesitantly walks on water.

Reference has already been made to Jesus' sovereign call of Peter (4:18-20), but it is well to note an additional point concerning Peter's occupation at the time of this encounter and the vocation to which Jesus now calls him and Andrew. In introducing these first two disciples Matthew describes them casting a net into the sea (presumably some form of hand net cast from the shore is understood) and relates that both had fishing as their work. Jesus calls them with these words: "Follow me and I will make you fishers for human beings" (4:19, author's translation).

The change in Peter's occupation that Jesus here effects takes on added significance when it is viewed in correlation with 16:17-19, the verses in which Jesus again effects a change in Peter's role. Here at 4:19 there is no change in Simon's name. Nevertheless, the call Jesus extends to him changes his work from the catching of fish to the work of fishing for, i.e., saving, human beings.

For Matthew's paradigmatic readers the placement of each of these passages, spotlighting Peter as Part II begins and as it closes, is intriguing.

In effect, Matthew has structured Part II of his Gospel in such a way that key episodes featuring Peter serve as "literary bookends" for Jesus' ministry.

In addition to these two bookend passages, Matthew references Peter in four other passages within Part II. After narrating the Sermon on the Mount and the healing of a leper and a centurion's servant, Matthew reports at 8:14-15 that Jesus "entered Peter's house" and "healed his mother-in-law lying sick with a fever." Inasmuch as Jesus does not visit the home of any other disciple and does not heal the relative of any other disciple, the import of this passage for suggesting a privileged relationship between Jesus and Peter is not negligible.[11]

Another passage in which Matthew highlights Peter's standing among the disciples (again without portraying any action on Peter's part) occurs at 10:2-4, where Simon's name is at the head of the list of apostles. In 10:2 Matthew also attests to what has been characterized as Simon's "firstness" by expressly placing the modifier "first" before his name.[12] As discussed above, at the end of this same verse Matthew adds the clause "who is called Peter" as a further amplification of Simon's identity.

Matthew 14:22-33, the passage to be treated next, requires extended exegesis. As a preliminary note it is useful to recall that, earlier in Matthew's narrative, Jesus has miraculously calmed a storm that was threatening the boat in which he and the disciples were traveling (8:23-27). In that earlier scene the term "little faith" occurred, and in that scene the disciples' fear was also a quality that exercised a considerable influence. Similarly, the concept of "little faith" and especially the concept of fear are both significant in the present scene.[13]

What is Matthew showing about Jesus in this passage? What is Matthew showing about Peter? These two basic questions should be kept in mind even in an initial reading of Matthew's carefully presented descriptions portraying how these two figures interacted so remarkably on the surface of the Sea of Galilee. Here, then, is Matthew's account:

> And in the fourth watch of the night he came to them, walking on the sea. But when the disciples saw him walking on the sea, they were terrified, saying, "It is a ghost!" And they cried out for fear. But immediately he spoke to them, saying, "Take heart, it is I; have no fear." And Peter answered him, "Lord, if it is you, bid me come to you on the water." He said, "Come." So Peter got out of the boat and walked on the water and came to Jesus; but when he saw the wind, he was afraid, and beginning to sink he cried out, "Lord, save me." Jesus immediately reached out his hand and caught him, saying to him, "O man of little faith, why did you doubt?" And when they got into the boat, the wind

ceased. And those in the boat worshiped him, saying, "Truly you are the Son of God." (14:25-33)

The exalted identity and sovereign power of Jesus are clearly evident in this passage. Jesus is indeed able to walk on water! What is more, he shares this power (for a time) with Peter. He also calms the turbulent winds just as he did in a previous episode at 8:23-27.

Jesus' characteristic benevolence toward his disciples can also be seen in this passage.[14] As Jesus proceeds across the waves to the disciples his sovereign power is manifest. But for what reason is Jesus heading toward his disciples? The text states that this event occurs during the fourth watch of the night, perhaps implying that Jesus, after many hours, is finally drawing near to assist his disciples. They have been rowing all night and have made scant progress against the powerful countervailing winds (14:24). If this interpretation be granted, then the particular solicitude Jesus will now show for Peter is situated within the context of Jesus' general benevolence toward his disciples. Perhaps the most difficult verse in this passage is 14:28, in which Peter boldly exclaims: "Lord, if it is you, bid me to come to you on the water." What precisely do these words mean?

As noted above Jesus has just declared with great sovereignty: "it is I; have no fear" (14:27b). Is there a question in Peter's mind as to whether this person is Jesus? Seemingly Peter knows that it is Jesus but is spontaneously seeking to verify if what his eyes tell him is true: that Jesus is walking on the water. The three short Greek words that constitute his response should thus probably be understood to mean: "If it is you *doing this*. . . ." Peter's words are intended to ascertain that Jesus really is walking on the water. If Jesus actually is doing this, then Peter wishes to join him.

Is there justification within Matthew's preceding narrative for the request Peter now makes? Consider briefly that Peter knows himself to be the first disciple Jesus has called to follow him (4:18-20). Remember that Peter has also experienced Jesus' particular favor when Jesus visited him and healed his mother-in-law (8:14-15). Recall also that Jesus has already entrusted a significant mission to Peter (and others) to heal the sick, raise the dead, cleanse lepers, and cast out demons (when the Twelve were sent out at 10:8). Note also that Peter has already faithfully accompanied his master through many situations of teaching and healing, situations in which Jesus' power has been dramatically manifested. In effect, given the character of Matthew's portrayal of him up to this point, Peter has good reason to be confident of Jesus' esteem for him.

In the interpretation now being proposed, Matthew's Peter now desires to share in this new manifestation of Jesus' sovereign power. Previously he has shared closely in the various dimensions of Jesus' ministry. He now (spontaneously) desires to share in this startling expression of Jesus' exalted status. And Jesus is agreeable to Peter's request. The factor of Jesus' favorable response looms larger the more carefully Matthew's narrative of this encounter is read. For absent Jesus' favorable response, Peter's request can be interpreted as braggadocio. It is only Jesus' favorable response that establishes Peter's bold request as appropriate.

Why is Jesus favorable to Peter's request? Why does he respond to Peter's entreaty with the unvarnished command: "Come!"? It is again important to read Matthew's present passage while keeping an eye on what has transpired between these two figures earlier in the narrative. The reverse side of Peter's experience in being chosen first by Jesus is that Jesus, for reasons Matthew does not disclose, decided to call Peter and Andrew before he called any of the other members of the Twelve. Further, the only home of a member of the Twelve that Jesus visited was the home of Peter. There he honored Peter by healing his mother-in-law from illness. Is there not already the beginning of a narrative pattern of Jesus' favorable interventions on Peter's behalf?

For any study of Peter in Matthew's Gospel, 14:29b is a momentous sentence: "So Peter got out of the boat and walked on the water and came to Jesus." Let a secondary spotlight focus on what Peter now accomplishes. How far away from the boat was Jesus when he gave Peter the command to come to him? How many yards? How many feet? Matthew is not so much interested in the distance covered as he is in the feat now being accomplished. Peter is actually walking on the water and approaching Jesus!

Fear then reappears. And this fear vitiates the faith Peter needs to keep if he is to complete his momentous journey and actually reach Jesus. Note that Matthew says nothing regarding any anticipation on Jesus' part regarding Peter's failure.[15] What Matthew does emphasize is that (a) Peter does fail and (b) Jesus does save him. In Matthew's vivid imagery Jesus immediately reaches out his hand and catches Peter. How far has Peter sunk before this occurs? Again Matthew is not so much interested in whether Peter sank up to his knees or his waist or his chest as he is in the fact that Jesus, still poised atop the waves, exercises his sovereign power and saves Peter from drowning.

In what tone of voice did Jesus then speak to Peter (14:31b): "O man of little faith, why did you doubt?" Does Matthew understand Jesus speaking with exasperation? With concern and gentleness? Or does Matthew understand these words to be spoken out of sadness?

If sadness is understood here, it is Jesus' sadness over Peter's tragic flaw of fear and its future consequences. In the present instance Jesus saves

Peter from the effect of his fear. But, as Matthew's paradigmatic readers grasp, this fear will have far more serious consequences in the future. Because of this fear Peter will later fail to stand by Jesus, and because of his engulfing fear he will deny Jesus three times.

Jesus' sovereignty permeates this entire episode and is appropriately responded to in the outcome of the scene. Jesus, clasping Peter, bestrides the stormy waves and these two eventually reach the boat and get into it. As they do so, the storm ceases. Those in the boat (and Peter is now present in this group) worship Jesus with a reverent confession of faith that is virtually the same as that of the centurion at Jesus' cross (14:33b; see 27:54c): "Truly you are the Son of God."

As noted previously, this acclamation of Jesus' exalted status as the Son of God precedes the acclamation of him as "the Christ, the Son of the living God" that Peter will make at 16:16. However, in comparison with the highly positive response he gives to Peter's later acclaim of him, Jesus makes no response to the disciples' present words of acclamation. Rather, Matthew simply presents Jesus continuing with the disciples in the boat until they land uneventfully at Gennesaret.

Two passages now remain to be considered in Matthew Part II. Brief attention will be given to Peter's request for a clarification in Matthew 15. In contrast, more extensive analysis will be required for Peter's confession and Jesus' response in Matthew 16 even though some aspects of this passage have already been considered above.

At 15:10-12, to the consternation of some Pharisees who are present, Jesus has set forth his teaching about the true source of defilement. At 15:15-20 Peter asks that Jesus "explain this parable to us," and Jesus does so, although not without first admonishing Peter and the others for their dullness (he uses "you" in the plural). Thus on the one hand Jesus does honor Peter's request, yet on the other hand he tenders the reproach: "Are you also still without understanding?"

Various aspects of the passage in which Jesus renames Peter and entrusts important new roles to him have been considered above in the section specifying that Jesus' mission included the founding of a church and in the section analyzing the meaning of Peter's name. Because of its importance for the overall interpretation of Peter in Matthew's Gospel,[16] this passage is now cited in full.

To make clear that Jesus is now addressing *solely* Peter, all of the singular pronouns referring to Peter will be italicized:

> Simon Peter replied, "You are the Christ, the Son of the living God." And Jesus answered him, "Blessed are *you*, Simon Bar-Jona! For flesh

> and blood has not revealed this to *you*, but my Father who is in heaven. And I tell *you*, *you* are Peter, and on this rock I will build my church, and the powers of death shall not prevail against it. I will give *you* the keys of the kingdom of heaven, and whatever *you* bind on earth shall be bound in heaven, and whatever *you* loose on earth shall be loosed in heaven." (Matt 16:16-19)

It was noted above that when the disciples (including Peter) worshiped and acclaimed Jesus, saying, "Truly, you are the Son of God" (14:33b), Jesus did not make any response. Now his response is spontaneously effusive. Is it Matthew's sense that Peter's prescient reply took Jesus by surprise? For seemingly there is a spontaneous dimension present in Jesus' response. It is as though Peter's acclamation is so well spoken that it immediately elicits from Jesus a highly affirmative response.

Jesus' reply is initially illumined when reference is made to an earlier Matthean passage in which Jesus uses the image of a rock. At 7:24-25 Jesus recommends to his disciples the benefits of building on rock. If they do indeed build their houses on rock, these buildings will be able to withstand the onslaught of rain and floods and violent winds.

In the setting of Matthew 7, building on rock remotely references disciples who put Jesus' teachings into practice and proximately references the conduct of a wise man. In Matthew 16 building on rock references Simon as the foundation rock for Jesus' church. Clearly, the reference points for "rock" are different in each passage. Nevertheless, in each case the benefit of building on rock is the same: what is built (a house; a church) is capable of withstanding buffeting from external forces (floods and winds; the gates of Hades). Further, when Matthew's paradigmatic readers consider the nuances of Matthew 16 in light of the nuances in Matthew 7, do they not interpret Jesus' endeavor to build his church on a rock foundation as the enterprise of a "wise" man?

Especially when they are considered in the light of 7:24-25, there is a tight logic to the steps that Matthew portrays Jesus taking at 16:16-19. As the ultimate endeavor of his ministry in Part II of the Gospel, Jesus now announces that he will build a church and indicates that Simon will serve this church in two important ways. Further, because one of the ways in which Simon will serve is as a rock of foundation, it is Jesus' desire that his name be changed to "Rock" (Peter).

Note that Jesus' initial blessing of Simon contributes to the tight logic of this passage. Because Simon alone has received a special revelation from Jesus' Father,[17] it is logically "plausible" that Simon alone should be singled out for this role. There is also a demonstrable logic in the renaming of Simon that Jesus now implements.

The fact that Jesus begins by formally addressing him as "Simon Bar-Jona" serves to focus attention on the renaming that will now occur. This renaming is an auxiliary step that supports Jesus' principal objective of establishing a church and his strategy of designating Simon as the rock foundation for this church. Giving Simon a new name that identifies his new role underscores the importance of the role.

If the words "you are Peter" were erased from Matthew's account of this episode, Jesus' initiative would still be intelligible: designating Simon to serve as the rock for Jesus' church. While Simon does not require a new name in order to fulfill his new commission, it is a part of Jesus' strategy for him henceforward to be known as "Rock."[18] To present this point in a slightly different way: if the idea of Jesus' church were removed from Matthew's narrative, there would be no need for any change of Simon's name to "Peter." Further, whenever the name "Peter" appears in Matthew's narrative there is always at least a minimal reference to "church." For without the foundation of a church there is no reason for the name "Peter" to exist.

In addition to functioning as a foundation rock for Jesus' church, Peter is also to function as a keeper of the keys of the kingdom of heaven, that is, as a steward. This second function and a brief explanation of how Peter will fulfill it is given in 16:19 and is appropriately reviewed at this point: "I will give *you* the keys of the kingdom of heaven and whatever *you* bind on earth shall be bound in heaven and whatever *you* loose on earth shall be loosed in heaven." Here again Jesus is sovereignly entrusting a significant role to Peter. Peter alone (the italicized occurrences of "you" in the preceding sentence indicate the second person singular) is being given keys that relate significantly to the kingdom of heaven. Whatever Peter himself binds and looses on earth shall be bound and loosed in heaven.

To what does this "binding" and "loosing" refer? There are at least two lines of interpretation regarding the meaning of these functions. The first focuses on Jesus' ministry of teaching in Matthew's Gospel. In the future (after Jesus' resurrection) Peter will share the role of authoritatively specifying the meaning and applicability of Jesus' teaching. The second interpretation focuses on church discipline. In the future Peter will have responsibility regarding the requirements for entering the church and the exigencies for exiting it. Certainly there is not a rigid demarcation between the lines of these two interpretations of "binding" and "loosing."

As discussed previously, Jesus gives this authority for binding and loosing to a group of disciples that includes Peter at Matthew 18:18. Because there is no counterpart to Matthew 16:19a in Matthew 18:18, Peter is the sole disciple imaged as holding the keys of the kingdom of heaven. However, based on 18:18, the ministry of "binding and loosing," the ministry of clarifying

Jesus' teaching and the role of determining church discipline, is one in which all the disciples share.

One final clause of Jesus' wording in Matthew 16:18-19 remains to be treated. It is a clause that predicates an enduring future for the church Jesus intends to build. A literal translation of the Greek words at 16:18b is: "and the gates of Hades will not prevail against it." Since the biblical writings generally use this expression to reference the realm of death, "the power of death" is the phrase the *RSV* translators have used for their translation.

This translation conveys Jesus' fundamental meaning: that his church will not fail and die, but rather will be safeguarded from disintegration and death. Jesus' reference to the future in this clause and his repeated reference to the future throughout Matthew 16:18-19 serve as indicators that his church is envisioned to extend into the future beyond the time of Jesus' own earthly ministry. Peter's ministry as a rock and as a steward entrusted with the keys of the kingdom of heaven presumably looks to this future. By Jesus' design his church is safeguarded from "the powers of death" and will continue into the future despite the events of Jesus' suffering and death. Further, as Matthew 28:20 will indicate, Jesus himself will continue to be present with his disciples "for all days, to the close of the age."

C. *Peter's Portrayal in Part III of Matthew's Gospel*

Two scenes in which Peter is highly prominent appear on either side of the divide between Part II and Part III of Matthew's Gospel. As Part II ended Peter reached his zenith as Jesus' disciple. However, only a few short verses into Part III he plummets precipitously. Nevertheless, despite this initial grievous decline, Peter's story in Part III is far from finished. He will have a speaking role in fully seven other scenes before Jesus' crucifixion and a graph of his discipleship will disclose that significant rising and falling remain in store for him before Part III is over.

Because Peter does appear as a key interlocutor with Jesus in so many of the scenes of Part III of the Gospel, it is useful to list these scenes at the outset before beginning the analysis of the first episode. They are as follows:

1. Peter's rejection of Jesus' suffering engenders Jesus' stern rebuke (16:21-23).
2. Peter (James and John) are with Jesus at his transfiguration (17:1-13).
3. Peter rashly presumes to answer regarding tax payments (17:24-27).

4. Peter asks about the extent of forgiveness (18:21-22).
5. Peter asks about the rewards for their discipleship (19:27).
6. Peter avows his faithfulness and Jesus predicts his denials (26:33-35).
7. Peter (James and John) are with Jesus at Gethsemane (26:36-46).
8. Peter denies Jesus three times and shows remorse (26:69-75).

As we make an initial approach to the opening scene in which Jesus castigates Peter as Satan, it is important to focus on the issue of the lapse of time within the story. Matthew's clause, "From that time Jesus began to show his disciples that he must go to Jerusalem and suffer many things . . ." (16:21a), marks a major divide between what has just occurred (Peter as blessed and a rock) and what happens next (Peter as Satanic and a stumbling block). Nevertheless, Matthew does not indicate whether Jesus waited minutes, hours, days, or weeks before decisively introducing the topic of his Passion and resurrection, which elicits Peter's agitated response.

What Matthew does make clear in terms of time intervals is that, as soon as Jesus broaches this topic, Peter immediately begins to try to dissuade him from the path of suffering:

> And Peter took him and began to rebuke him, saying, "God forbid, Lord! This shall never happen to you." But he turned and said to Peter, "Get behind me, Satan! You are a stumbling block to me; for you are not on the side of God, but of human beings." (Matt 16:22-23, author's translation)

From zenith standing to nadir standing! Formerly Simon was especially blessed because the Father had entrusted a privileged revelation to him. Now he is a serious threat to Jesus' mission. Formerly he merited the new name of "Peter." Now he bears the name of "Satan."[19]

The presence of the word "stumbling block" in the present passage also effectively emphasizes the magnitude of Peter's decline. This word bears a conceptual affinity with "rock," the term Jesus uses at 16:18 to indicate the new role and name Simon will have. In effect Jesus now castigates him for becoming the opposite of a "foundation rock" for Jesus' church. Far from functioning positively, Peter is actually functioning negatively. Far from fulfilling the stabilizing role Jesus intends for him, Peter ("Satan") is now fulfilling a destabilizing role, functioning as an "obstacle rock" over which Jesus himself can stumble.

What is Peter's reaction to the chastisement Jesus visits upon him? No reaction whatsoever is described within Matthew's narrative at this point. Subsequently Jesus elaborates for all his disciples, Peter presumably included, that self-denial and cross-embrace will be required for those who follow him (16:24-28). At this point Peter does not dissent from this new teaching regarding discipleship, yet neither does Matthew portray him affirming it.

"After six days . . .," Matthew's subsequent clause, indicates that a significant interval of time passes before the next event that occurs. Jesus now invites Peter, James, and John to join him on a high mountain and to be witnesses of his transfiguration. What does the inclusion of Peter in this group indicate? Is not the implicit logic of Matthew's narrative that Jesus no longer regards him as "Satanic"?

Peter, in fact, functions in a significantly positive fashion as Matthew's description of this event unfolds. When Jesus is transfigured and Moses and Elijah appear with him, the awestruck Peter addresses Jesus as "Lord" and deferentially proposes to build three dwellings: "if you wish, I will make three booths here" (17:4). Here Peter is the only one of the three disciples to speak and his use of the first person singular seems to imply that he will construct the three booths by himself.

As Matthew's narrative of this scene unfolds, all three disciples fall fearfully to the ground when they hear the heavenly voice from the cloud. They are "filled with awe" but also influenced by fear until Jesus touches them reassuringly and bids them rise (17:6-8). Peter is not mentioned by name as the party of four then descends the mountain, but he is implicitly included when Matthew relates that the disciples conversed with Jesus about Elijah and drew the inference that Jesus identified Elijah with John the Baptist (17:10-13).

In terms of Peter's "trajectory," Matthew's presentation of the Transfiguration discloses that Peter's roles as "Satan" and "stumbling block" have been a temporary phenomenon. Peter now again enjoys a significant intimacy with Jesus and again functions prominently within Jesus' especially favored group of three. While he and the two brothers have not been free from fear during the Transfiguration, they have manifested appropriate awe and Jesus himself has assisted them in overcoming their fear.

If Matthew's transfiguration narrative depicts Peter's return to grace and portrays him speaking out in an appropriate manner, Peter's performances in two of the next three scenes in which he speaks out do not match the high level of his performance at the Transfiguration.

At 17:24-27 collectors of a *Roman* tax approach Peter to ask him whether Jesus pays this tax. Here Matthew images Peter as someone who can be approached for an interpretation of Jesus' practice. Peter's straightforward answer is that Jesus does pay the tax. However, as the scene unfolds this answer turns out to be unsatisfactory to Jesus. Jesus' precise approach to the payment of this tax is veiled behind an epigrammatic comment and a directive to pursue an astonishing solution. What is clearly evident is that Jesus will not allow Peter's simple "yes" to stand as representative of his (Jesus') position. Nevertheless, although Peter has been mistaken, Jesus, in the end, still benevolently and wondrously arranges for Peter's own tax to be paid.[20]

In somewhat parallel fashion Peter's attempt to render Jesus' position on forgiveness is also judged by Jesus to be inaccurate. In this instance Peter asks Jesus whether it is appropriate to place a limit of seven times upon forgiveness (18:21-22). As in the case of the question concerning taxation, Jesus corrects the answer Peter has proposed. Jesus' actual position is that the willingness to forgive shall be "seventy times seven," that is, unlimited. From one perspective Peter's initially incorrect response serves positively in that the full character of Jesus' teaching is now clarified for the benefit of all.

In the third case in which Peter speaks out, Jesus responds positively to the concern Peter voices. To the rich young man's question, Jesus has enunciated a startling teaching concerning the great difficulty the rich will have in entering the kingdom of heaven (19:16-24). The disciples as a group are shocked by this teaching, but Jesus clarifies that all things are possible with God. Peter then asks (19:27): "Lo, we have left everything to follow you. What then shall we have?" Jesus receives this question with favor and predicts to the entire group of disciples that they will sit on twelve thrones judging the twelve tribes of Israel. (This instance of external predictive prolepsis has already been noted.) Further, anyone leaving relatives or land for Jesus' sake will receive both a hundredfold and eternal life (19:28-30).

From this point forward Peter does not appear by name until 26:33. Implicitly he is present when Jesus announces to the disciples as a group that they are now going up to Jerusalem, where Jesus will be delivered to condemnation and death and then rise again. This is the third major Passion prediction in Matthew's Gospel (20:17-19). Implicitly Peter is also present with other disciples in the various Jerusalem scenes and teachings Matthew delineates. He then re-emerges prominently at the Last Supper when he reacts strongly to Jesus' prediction that the disciples will all fall away from him (26:31).

To his words regarding the disciples' desertion Jesus appends the significant prediction: "But after I am raised up I will go before you to Galilee" (26:32). However, Peter's response to Jesus' words only addresses the first of these two predictions: Peter avows that he himself will never fall away!

In many respects Peter's response represents the highwater mark of his discipleship in Matthew. His earlier high achievement was to confess Jesus as the Christ (16:16). Now he seemingly surpasses that achievement by expressing an intensely personal commitment never to abandon Jesus. Yet as the narrative unfolds, Peter will not prove faithful to Jesus. Jesus, knowing this, will not allow Peter's laudable declaration to remain unchallenged even for a moment. He immediately predicts Peter's threefold denial.

In contrast with his silence in the previous case, when he received the devastating "Satan" and "stumbling block" rebuke from Jesus, Peter is not silent here. Rather, he boldly counters Jesus' prediction, avowing his faithfulness even to death! Jesus does not now make a further response. Peter's bravado notwithstanding, the truth of Jesus' prediction will become evident in only a few short hours. Here, then, is this truly remarkable exchange between Jesus and his outspoken disciple:

> But Peter declared to him, "Though they all fall away because of you, I will never fall away." Jesus said to him, "Truly, I say to you, this very night before the cock crows, you will deny me three times." Peter said to him, "Even if I must die with you, I will not deny you." And so said all the disciples. (Matt 26:33-35)

It is clear from what Matthew has just related that when Jesus now leads his disciples toward Gethsemane he knows full well that Peter's pledge of allegiance will turn out to be bankrupt. Nevertheless, once he arrives in the garden Jesus departs from the larger group of disciples in order to pray, taking with him only Peter (!), who is named, and the two sons of Zebedee. (Recall that these are the same three disciples Jesus invited to be with him at the Transfiguration.) Bidding these three to keep watch, Jesus goes a distance apart to pray intensely, but then returns to find them sleeping (26:38-40a).

According to Matthew's next report, Jesus then reproaches Peter directly, referring to the fact that all three have failed to keep watch. Even though Jesus again expressly asks them to watch and pray, he subsequently returns to find them sleeping a second time. This sequence then repeats itself a third time, right to the point at which the arresting party draws near. In terms of Matthew's portrayal of Peter, this sequence in which Peter three times fails to "watch and pray" (26:36-45) can be regarded as a narrative anticipation of the far more serious three denials that are still to come. In reporting this sequence, at 26:43b, Matthew offers the slightly exculpatory comment: "for their eyes were heavy." There will be no such exonerating reference when Peter makes his denials.

In fulfillment of Jesus' first prophecy, all of his disciples do eventually forsake him and flee once he is apprehended (26:56). Nevertheless, Peter follows "at a distance" into the courtyard of the high priest (26:58). While Jesus is being interrogated, Peter fulfills Jesus' second prophecy by denying him three times (26:69-74). There is a noteworthy crescendo to these denials. When first challenged by a maid, Peter denies before everyone present that he was with Jesus, blustering that he does not understand what the maid is talking about (26:69-70). When accosted by a second maid, Peter uses an oath to buttress his claim that he doesn't even *know* Jesus (26:72). Finally, when one of the bystanders cites Peter's accent as an indication that Peter is one of Jesus' group, Peter invokes a *curse* upon himself to strengthen his oath that "I do not know the man" (26:74). After this third denial, the cock crows.

When Part III of the Gospel opened, Peter plummeted precipitously from his zenith standing, becoming "Satan" and "a stumbling block." Next in order, Jesus took the initiative in restoring Peter to high standing by inviting him to participate in the Transfiguration. In the following interval of Jesus' unfolding ministry Matthew portrayed Peter speaking out in three instances, with mixed results. In two cases he rendered Jesus' position incorrectly. Nevertheless, in the third case his question provided the occasion for Jesus' positive response that the Twelve would sit upon thrones judging the twelve tribes of Israel.

Peter's second sheer descent is now at hand. Peter still stands on high ground at the Mout of Olives: He proclaims that he will never fall away from Jesus and that he will die with him before denying him. For his part, even though he is convinced of (and has predicted) Peter's desertion and denial, Jesus still invites Peter, along with James and John, to witness his intimate prayer at Gethsemane. It is in Gethsemane that Peter's precipitous descent begins.

First Peter cannot remain awake while Jesus is praying. Then he actually joins the other disciples in forsaking Jesus and fleeing from the arresting party. Finally, despite trying to recover his standing as Jesus' disciple by following Jesus to the high priest's courtyard, Peter ultimately distances, distances, distances himself from Jesus through his three denials.

Jesus has sovereignly intervened on Peter's behalf earlier in Matthew's narrative. What will happen now? Matthew initially provides a slight hint of yet another restoration for Peter when he states that, after the cock's crow, "Peter remembered the saying of Jesus . . . and he went out and wept bitterly" (26:75).[21]

It is important to note that this expression of sorrow does not galvanize Peter to resume following Jesus when Jesus is led away to the trial before the Roman governor. Nor does Matthew indicate that Peter (or any of the eleven) found courage to keep Jesus in sight at his crucifixion. Peter is thus clearly at the low point of his discipleship as Part III approaches its final scenes. Do Peter's sorrow and his tears imply that he has not yet reached the final stage of his trajectory as Jesus' disciple? The answer to this question must be sought within the resurrection scenes that close Part III of the Gospel.

5. Peter and the Risen Jesus

In Matthew's resurrection narrative Mary Magdalene and "the other Mary" are the only disciples of Jesus mentioned by name. As these two women near the tomb of Jesus, the phenomena of a great earthquake and an angel rolling back the stone occur (28:1-2). The women then receive the angel's announcement of Jesus' resurrection (28:5-7), and in their joy they are privileged to behold the risen Jesus (28:9).

What about Peter, last seen in the narrative bitterly weeping? Do the wording of the angel's announcement to the women and then the risen Jesus' instructions to them both imply that Peter and the other ten members of the Twelve are gathered somewhere as a group? Recall that Matthew has not indicated Peter's location or the location of the other ten during the events of Jesus' crucifixion and burial.

In part, the angel instructs the women: "go quickly and tell his disciples . . . behold he is going before you to Galilee; there you will see him" (28:7). Jesus' words similarly imply a reunion in Galilee: "go and tell my brethren to go to Galilee, and there they will see me" (28:10b).

Matthew's narrative now proceeds to its closing scene, the memorable setting of the mountain in Galilee referenced at the very outset of the present chapter. These verses feature Jesus' auspicious closing comments to the members of the eleven (neither Peter nor any members of the eleven are named), in which he commissions them for the future work of making disciples of all nations. Peter's participation in this scene represents the final instance within the Gospel in which Jesus restores him to high standing. By reason of their own participation in this scene, the other members of the eleven are similarly restored. Recall that in their last appearance within the narrative these others were fleeing from Jesus' side at the time of his arrest (26:56b).

Specifically, on drawing near to the eleven, some of whom evidence uncertainty regarding his identity, Jesus solemnly commissions them for their future ministry of making disciples of all nations. They are to accomplish this "discipling" through a ministry of baptizing and teaching; for the first time in the Gospel they are now authorized to teach. The final verse of Matthew's Gospel contains a dimension of prediction and one of reassuring promise: Jesus will continue to remain with all his disciples for "all days, to the close of the age."

6. Summary of Matthew's Portrayal of Peter

In Part II of his Gospel Matthew portrays Jesus calling Peter first and underscores Peter's prominence on the list of Jesus' selected apostles by employing the modifier "first." In various episodes Peter enjoys a privileged closeness with Jesus and is even accorded the privilege of walking on water. Along with others, Peter is subject to having "little faith." Nevertheless, as Part II closes he reaches his zenith by confessing that Jesus is the Christ. Jesus' response to Simon's confession is to bestow on him the name "Peter," a name linked with this disciple's new role in serving as a rock foundation for Jesus' church.

At the beginning of Part III, Peter tries to dissuade Jesus from the path of suffering and death. In reply Jesus castigates him as "Satan" and calls him a "stumbling block." Nevertheless, Jesus then restores Peter by inviting him to experience his transfiguration. Peter then continues to follow Jesus and, along with the other apostles, eventually receives the promise that he will serve as a judge over the twelve tribes of Israel. As Jesus' Passion draws near, Peter proclaims his willingness to die with him. Yet he is unable to stay awake in Gethsemane and he egregiously denies Jesus three times in the high priest's courtyard.

Peter's tears of repentance represent an initial step in his return to faithful discipleship, but full restoration does not occur until the risen Jesus gathers him and the rest of the eleven in Galilee. In a mountain setting Jesus majestically imparts to them a mandate for making disciples of all nations. Matthew, having previously emphasized Jesus' multiple initiatives on behalf of Peter, does not mention him by name in these post-resurrection scenes.

Summary of Peter's Trajectory and Predicted Future in Matthew

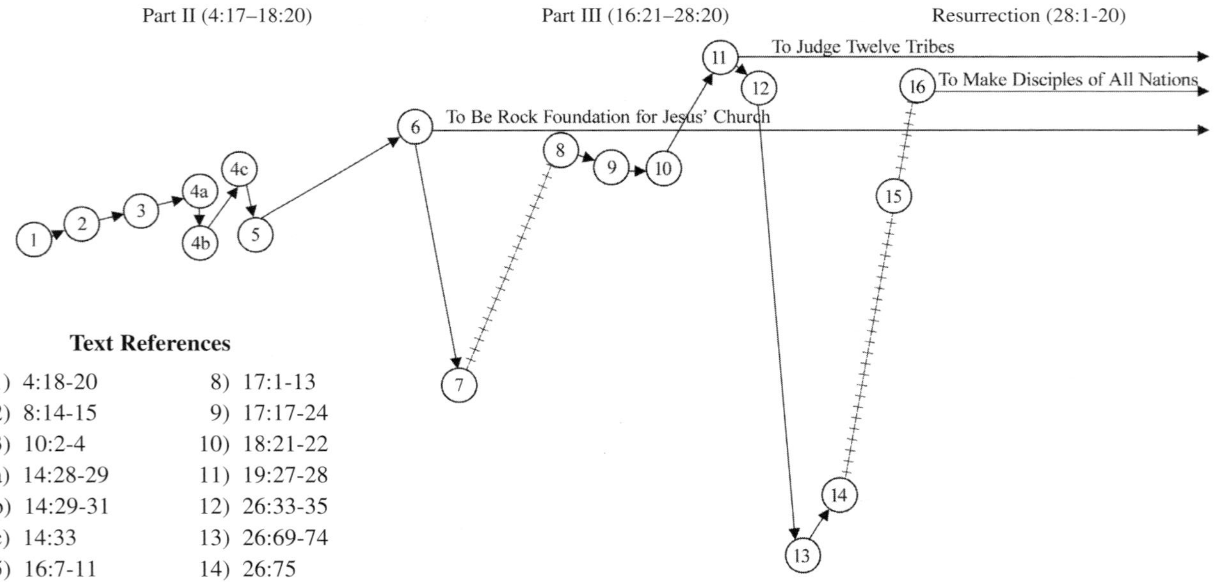

Text References

1)	4:18-20	8)	17:1-13
2)	8:14-15	9)	17:17-24
3)	10:2-4	10)	18:21-22
4a)	14:28-29	11)	19:27-28
4b)	14:29-31	12)	26:33-35
4c)	14:33	13)	26:69-74
5)	16:7-11	14)	26:75
6)	16:16-19	15)	28:7
7)	16:22-23	16)	28:16-20

+ + + + Emphasizes Jesus' Sovereign Intervention

CHAPTER FIVE

Peter in John's Gospel: From Hireling to Jesus' Good Shepherd

The first section of this chapter will briefly note that John's Gospel projects a future for Peter that extends beyond the Gospel's final scene. The second section will then analyze John's overall presentation regarding Jesus and his mission. Section three will take up the topic of John's general portrayal of Jesus' disciples. In section four an analysis will be made regarding the Beloved Disciple, a figure unique to John's Gospel. Sections five and six will then present an extended analysis of how Peter himself is portrayed within this Gospel.

1. The Future-Oriented Character of John's Gospel

In John's Gospel Jesus repeatedly stresses that he is only in the world for a short time and that when his "hour" arrives he will depart and return to the Father. In the words he imparts to his disciples at the time of their final supper together Jesus is manifestly concerned to prepare these disciples to withstand the persecution they will face after his departure. Then, in chapters 20 and 21 of the Gospel, the risen Jesus entrusts to his disciples various ministries that they, empowered by the Spirit, will exercise in the future on his behalf.

2. Jesus and his Mission According to John[1]

As portrayed in the Gospel of John, the mission of Jesus has fundamentally to do with belief. Jesus has been sent by the Father to invite belief in himself as the only-begotten Son of God so that those who come to believe will have life in his name (20:31). At his appointed hour Jesus will return to the Father and will effect the sending of the Holy Spirit. However, during the interval in which he is present in the world the central emphasis of his ministry is to invite others to believe in *him.*

This he does principally by means of signs and discourses. Seven major signs can be identified within the interval of public ministry, with the restoration of Lazarus to life as the seventh and culminating sign (11:1-44). While the signs confer a benefit on those who are the recipients of Jesus' interventions, the primary purpose of each sign is to manifest the sovereignty of Jesus and thus to occasion belief in him.

In his narrative of Jesus' public ministry John portrays Jesus traveling back and forth between Galilee and Judea, with frequent participation at the major Jewish feasts including three observances of Passover. In virtually every episode that occurs during his travels and his participation at these feasts, Jesus in one way or another calls upon those he encounters to believe in him (for example, at 3:15; 8:30; 10:25-26). Many of those who hear his discourses and witness his signs do come to belief. Yet almost from the outset of the narrative a serious opposition to Jesus' claims is manifested by an alliance of chief priests and Pharisees that John frequently characterizes as "the Jews."[2]

Jesus presents himself to these adversaries, as well as to the Jews who believe in him, as the one who replaces worship at the Jerusalem Temple and the observance of the Jewish Law. He is the one whom Moses desired to see and, even more astoundingly, he is the one who existed before Abraham came to be (8:58). Jesus is, after all, the beloved Son of the Father (1:18). Further, using imagery that will reappear in new form in the final scene of the Gospel, Jesus images himself as the Good Shepherd who tenderly cares for his sheep even to the point of laying down his life for them (10:2-18, 27-30).

Threatened by the popular impact of Jesus' signs, and galvanized especially by the raising of Lazarus, the chief priests and their allies, led by Caiaphas, formally begin to seek Jesus' death (11:47-53). (Prior to this formal decision Jesus' inflammatory words have engendered several unsuccessful spontaneous attempts to apprehend and/or stone him.) John presents Jesus as being fully aware of his enemies' plans and fully cognizant of the role Judas will play against him (13:21). Because Jesus is in constant communion with his heavenly Father, nothing that occurs takes him by surprise (18:4). Nor is there anything that occurs in his arrest, trial, and crucifixion to which Jesus does not consent.

This Johannine feature of Jesus' sovereignty over his enemies is perhaps most evident at the time of his arrest. When Jesus identifies himself to the arresting party by using words expressive of his divinity, *egō eimi* (literally

"I am"), those striving to arrest him fall to the ground stunned (18:5-6). John's portrayal of Jesus before Pilate continues to manifest the theme of Jesus' unqualified sovereignty. John portrays Jesus engaging Pilate with such self-possession that, within John's narrative, Pilate himself seems the one on trial!

Another distinctive feature of John's trial narrative is the elaborate set of interactions between Pilate and Jesus' prosecutors, the chief priests and the Pharisees. In the end Caiaphas and his allies work the precise lever that is needed to secure the governor's compliance: Pilate's concern for his own career (19:12). Lest he lose his own status and aspirations to be a "Friend of Caesar," Pilate orders Jesus' crucifixion as the "King of the Jews" (19:19).

These last two political identifications contribute to John's emphasis on Jesus' surpassing sovereignty. In addition to ascribing the titles "King" and "Lord" to Jesus, the Gospel also attributes two other titles of sovereignty to him. At 4:42 the Samaritan townspeople momentously acclaim him as "the Savior of the world." Then, at the high summit of chapter 20, Thomas magnanimously addresses him with the appellation "my Lord and my God" (20:28).

When Jesus has ascended the cross and completed his mission he announces solemnly: "It is finished" (19:30). What remains in the Gospel narrative is for Jesus to commission his disciples, Peter prominently included, for their own future ministries on Jesus' behalf. In John 20–21 the risen Jesus describes a significant number of such ministries.

3. The Disciples of Jesus in John[3]

As indicated in the preceding section, John's Gospel is fundamentally concentrated on the person and mission of Jesus. The first subsection below will briefly consider the sovereignty with which Jesus calls his named (and unnamed) disciples. The second subsection will then identify Jesus' named disciples and consider the general features of the response he expects from them. The third subsection will present a general evaluation of the performance of these disciples as a means of preparing for a later evaluation of the performances of the Beloved Disciple and Peter.

A. *Jesus' Pre-eminence*

John's general emphasis on Jesus' exalted identity is consistently carried through in his descriptions of how Jesus selects and orients his disciples. One passage that decisively establishes Jesus' pre-eminent role occurs within the discourses of the Last Supper. As part of the reflections and teachings

Jesus shared with his disciples that evening, he expressly reminds them that they came to be his followers precisely because of Jesus' own initiative (15:16a): "You did not choose me, but I chose you. . . ."

B. *The Call to Discipleship in John's Gospel*

At the beginning of this section treating discipleship in general it is useful to provide a preliminary indication of how large Peter looms within John's overall narrative. Peter's words are quoted thirteen times in five different scenes in the Gospel, including six instances of recorded speech at the Last Supper.[4]

Within John's Gospel two of John the Baptist's disciples are directed by the Baptist to Jesus and subsequently become Jesus' first disciples. One of the two is not named; the other is Andrew. Jesus calls both these individuals, majestically inviting them to "come and see" (1:39a). Significantly, Andrew then locates his brother Simon (Peter) and testifies to him (1:41), "We have found the Messiah." Andrew brings Simon to Jesus. According to John 1:42, Jesus already knows Simon's identity and discloses that to him before affirming that his name will now be changed to Cephas and Peter.

The next day, when Jesus gains two additional disciples, his full command of each situation is apparent. Jesus himself "finds" Philip and tells him to "follow me." In a way somewhat parallel to Andrew's approach in inviting Peter, Philip then invites Nathaniel (1:45-46). Jesus' response to Nathaniel continues in the vein of his previous response to Peter but is even more reflective of his sovereign power. To Nathaniel's astonishment, Jesus says that he has already seen him and knows his character. Nathaniel replies with a resounding acclamation that rivals Andrew's proclamation to Peter for its high christology (1:49): "Rabbi, you are the Son of God! You are the king of Israel!"

These, then, are Jesus' first five disciples according to John. John 6:67 will subsequently clarify that there is a group of twelve disciples with whom Jesus is closely associated. Nevertheless, the precise membership of this group is never identified. Peter can be presumed to be a member of the Twelve (6:68); Judas Iscariot (6:71) and Thomas (20:24) are also members of this group. Nevertheless, many of the individual disciples who are prominent within John's narrative (for example, Andrew, Philip, Lazarus, and the Beloved Disciple) are never explicitly identified as members of this group.

What precise response does Jesus desire from his first five disciples? During the time of his public mission Jesus' disciples are fundamentally asked to believe in him, to follow him, and to remain with him. These concepts of believing and following are intertwined in the calling of Andrew, the unnamed disciple, Philip, and Nathaniel within the narrative of John's first chapter and they continue to be key facets for all those who come to be Jesus' disciples from that point forward.

A brief consideration of John's account of the wedding at Cana serves to clarify the role of Jesus' disciples in following and believing in him. This passage also provides an introduction to John's characteristic generalized references to "the disciples," references that make it difficult to determine the number or the identities of those who are being referred to. At 2:2 John states that Jesus was invited to the marriage "with his disciples." At the end of this episode, in which Jesus has responded to his mother's request by transforming water into wine, John summarizes as follows: "This, the first of his signs, Jesus did at Cana in Galilee, and manifested his glory; and *his disciples believed in him*" (2:11; emphasis added). Who are the individuals referenced at 2:2 and 2:11 under the general term "his disciples"? It may be inferred that this designation encompasses the five disciples called in John's first chapter. They are now following Jesus and are continuing to believe in him.

In his next report John states that "his disciples" journeyed to Capernaum with Jesus and his mother and brothers (2:12). "His disciples" are then said to be with Jesus in Jerusalem for the next episode of his public ministry, his protest at the Temple (2:22). John now indicates that "many," presumably many others beyond those called at the outset, believed in Jesus' name. Nevertheless, because of his ability to search into the depths of human beings Jesus did not trust himself to all in this group (2:24). Jesus then encounters Nicodemus and discourses extensively about the importance of belief and the phenomenon of being born again (3:1-15). John's next transition report is: "After this Jesus *and his disciples* went into the land of Judea" (3:22a; emphasis added). In the next episode, the encounter with the Samaritan woman, Jesus' disciples are with him; however, in the two following episodes, the healing of the official's son in Galilee and the curing of the crippled man in Jerusalem, John spotlights only Jesus and does not mention the presence of his disciples.

In chapter 6, for the sign of the multiplication of the loaves, a group of disciples is at Jesus' side, and in this instance John expressly indicates that Philip and Andrew, two of the first five called, are a part of the group. But who else does John understand to be included? This issue becomes even more complex when Jesus' fifth sign, the miraculous walking on water, is considered. This sign is sandwiched between the action of the multiplication of the loaves (6:1-15) and the discourse articulating that Jesus is truly the bread of life (6:22-71). In this sign Jesus walks on the water toward a group of his disciples who are rowing in a rising sea with heavy winds. In a display of his sovereign power, Jesus calms the turbulent sea and these disciples are glad to take him into their boat (6:20-21). Once again John's focus is so much on Jesus that he does not disclose the identities of the disciples who are present in the boat.

Nevertheless, in the controversy that ensues in the aftermath of Jesus' bread of life discourse it does become clear that more disciples than the original five are now following Jesus and believing in him. At 6:60 John reports that "many of his disciples" challenged Jesus' teaching regarding his saying that he himself is the bread of life to be eaten. Jesus' response to this challenge is to declare that some disciples are now failing to believe (6:64-65). The next verses in John's account have been said to describe "the Galilean crisis," a term that is appropriate as long as it is recognized that this crisis is one of belief, not one pertaining to Jesus' confidence in his mission. It is useful to cite these verses in their entirety:

> After this many of his disciples drew back and no longer went about with him. Jesus said to the twelve, "Do you also wish to go away?" Simon Peter answered him, "Lord, to whom shall we go? You have the words of eternal life: and we have believed, and have come to know that you are the Holy One of God." Jesus answered them, "Did I not choose you, the twelve, and one of you is a devil?" He spoke of Judas the son of Simon Iscariot, for he, one of the twelve, was to betray him. (John 6:66-71)

In the following section focused consideration will be given to the response given by Peter in this passage. Here the focus is on the standing of "the Twelve" within Jesus' larger group of disciples. Note that when John's report that "many of his disciples drew back and no longer went around with him" is contrasted with Jesus' query to the Twelve, it emerges logically that the total number of Jesus' disciples implied by this passage is larger than has been indicated within John's narrative up to this point.

This passage also implies the "the Twelve" constitute a distinct subset within the larger group of Jesus' disciples. Jesus' words indicate that he personally chose the members of the Twelve and indicate consternation that one of them "is a devil." In the remainder of the Gospel there is only one additional reference to this group. At 20:24 the phrase "one of *the twelve*" is used along with the phrase "called the Twin" as a means of identifying Thomas.

In his Last Supper discourses Jesus identifies new standards of behavior for his disciples. During the preceding years of Jesus' public mission these requirements have not been expressly specified; they are set forth now as the "hour" of Jesus' return to the Father draws near. Jesus expressly challenges his disciples to wash one another's feet (13:14) and to love one another as he has loved them (13:34; 15:12, 17). He also prays expressly for their internal unity (17:20-22) and advises them that, after his departure, others will believe in him "through their word" (17:20b).

What is more, after his departure the disciples can expect persecution from the religious authorities (15:20; 16:2a; 16:33) and even martyrdom from the political authorities (16:2b). Nevertheless, Jesus' departure will not leave them resourceless. Jesus and the Father will send the Holy Spirit, the Paraclete, as a powerful agent for their strengthening (14:15-17; 14:25-26; 15:26-27; 16:7-15).

Who precisely are present to receive this teaching and this mission? In addition to Peter, the Beloved Disciple, and Judas Iscariot, Thomas (14:5), Philip (14:8-9), and Judas not Iscariot (14:22) are expressly mentioned. How many other disciples does John understand to be present at this supper? At 18:1b John does not identify or indicate the number of those who depart with Jesus for the garden on the other side of the Kidron valley. In the subsequent events of the arrest and initial interrogation of Jesus, Judas and Peter are the only disciples mentioned by name.

C. *Assessing the Performance of Jesus' Disciples*

How shall the performance of Jesus' disciples in the Gospel of John be assessed? Such an evaluation must reflect the particular character of Jesus' requirements for his disciples and also take account of his intervention on their behalf at the time of his arrest. In addition, brief consideration must also be given to the emergence of the Beloved Disciple, along with the Mother of Jesus, at the foot of Jesus' cross.

Jesus' disciples are fundamentally required to believe in him, to follow him, and to remain with him. How well do they fulfill these requirements? The performance of the disciples at 6:66-71 has already been discussed. The other key passage to be considered occurs at the time of his arrest when Jesus speaks the following words (18:8): "I told you that I am he; so, if you seek me, let these men go." The ramifications of this latter verse for an evaluation of the disciples' performance will now be considered.

As events subsequently unfold, only Peter who will deny him and another unnamed disciple (who may be the Beloved Disciple; see below) follow Jesus. However, while the rest of his disciples do not *follow* Jesus, John's overall presentation may indicate that they are still desirous of *remaining* with him. In effect, because Jesus authoritatively orders that they be let go, the failure of the disciples who do not follow him is not as great as if they had simply fled. Nevertheless, the Beloved Disciple's steadfast example of following Jesus to the cross (and his remaining there with Jesus' mother) represents a strong contrast with the degree of believing and remaining that is characteristic of the other disciples, including Peter, who are not present in this momentous scene.

In overseeing his burial, Joseph of Arimathea also emerges as a disciple who *remains* with Jesus in an extraordinary way, even though the evangelist does qualify that Joseph's fear had kept him from being a public disciple until this time (19:38). The presence of other women at the cross (19:25) along with the mother of Jesus and the Beloved Disciple is yet another example of the complex way in which John presents his overall themes of believing and remaining.

In summary, John's Gospel supplies a generally favorable portrayal of the performance of Jesus' closest disciples (Peter's performance is a special case). Fundamentally, the disciples are dependent on Jesus to withstand "the hour of darkness" that commences with Judas' betrayal. Jesus decisively intervenes to prevent this crisis from damaging his disciples. They do not have to decide whether to remain or flee because Jesus immediately opens a passage for their safe conduct. Note, however, that those whom Jesus protects do not reappear publicly as his committed disciples until the Resurrection has occurred.

4. The Beloved Disciple[5]

Any effort to assess the portrayal of Peter in John's Gospel necessarily also involves a consideration of the portrayal of another prominent disciple. This disciple is identified as "the disciple whom Jesus loved" in the Greek and is commonly referred to as "the Beloved Disciple" in English-language commentaries. The Beloved Disciple is explicitly referenced at five points of the Gospel narrative (13:23-24; 19:26; 20:2-3; 21:7; 21:20-21) and he may be implicitly referenced at 1:35 and 18:15. Each of the scenes in which this disciple appears deserves careful consideration, especially so the four scenes in which he is shown interacting with Peter.

When the Beloved Disciple first explicitly appears in John's narrative, he comes with high status. John describes the position of this disciple at the farewell supper in the following terms (13:23): "One of his disciples, whom Jesus loved, was lying close to the breast of Jesus. . . ." This description recalls John's portrayal of the Son reclining in the bosom of the Father (1:18) and urges John's paradigmatic readers to consider whether the Beloved Disciple is as intimate with Jesus as Jesus is with the Father.[6]

Peter's high estimation of the Beloved Disciple's rapport with Jesus proves to be well founded. In response to Peter's request, this disciple asks Jesus (13:25): "Lord, who is it?" From Jesus' spoken and gestured response, the Beloved Disciple learns that Judas is the betrayer (13:26), but the evangelist does not portray him communicating this knowledge back to Peter. As Judas departs, and even until the scene of the arrest in the garden, Jesus and the Beloved Disciple are presumably the only two who know that Judas is Jesus' betrayer.

The next scene in which the Beloved Disciple is explicitly named is the scene at the foot of the cross (19:25-27). Does John understand this disciple to be present in one of the intervening scenes between the Last Supper and the cross, specifically the scene in the high priest's courtyard? The evangelist states only that "another disciple," someone "known to the high priest" enters the high priest's courtyard along with Jesus (18:15). This disciple then arranges for Peter to enter the courtyard (18:16). Because this figure shows a remarkable tenacity in following Jesus and remaining with him (the same qualities the Beloved Disciple evidences in being present at the cross), John's paradigmatic readers may judge that these two disciples are one and the same.

At 19:25 the evangelist indicates that the mother of Jesus and at least two other women are standing with the Beloved Disciple near the cross of Jesus. Given the Gospel's emphasis on believing, following, and remaining, all the members of the gathered group are cast in a favorable light. This is especially the case for the Beloved Disciple, who has demonstrated a consistent following of Jesus from the Last Supper to the garden of Jesus' arrest, and now to the cross of his "lifting up." Indeed, this disciple is the premier figure in the Gospel of John for modeling a sustained, uncompromised response to Jesus.

If the presence of the Beloved Disciple at the cross is significant in terms of his remaining, it is all the more significant that Jesus then selects this disciple to enter into a filial role with Jesus' own mother. Jesus first says to his mother: "Woman, behold your son," and then to this disciple, "Behold your mother" (19:26b). In effect, Jesus' words bring a new family into being. The Beloved Disciple's response to Jesus' directive is that of a model son:[7] "And from that hour the disciple took her to his own home." Note that this step reveals both a present and a future orientation. This is a consideration that bears upon the constellation of ministries the Beloved Disciple and Peter are charged with fulfilling into the future.

The third scene in which the Beloved Disciple is explicitly portrayed is again one in which he interacts with Peter. In 20:2-10, after Mary Magdalene has run to them bringing the news of Jesus' empty tomb, Peter and the

Beloved Disciple set out together running toward the tomb. Outrunning Peter, the Beloved Disciple reaches the site first and has time to make a preliminary inspection from outside the tomb.

Because the Beloved Disciple has waited for him, Peter is the first to enter the empty tomb. He observes the burial cloths and the cover from Jesus' head lying separately from the cloths, but the evangelist does not portray Peter coming to belief as a result of his viewing of the evidence. In contrast, when the Beloved Disciple entered the tomb "he saw and *believed*" (20:8b; emphasis added). In effect, the Beloved Disciple has been able to interpret correctly the evidence given by the arrangement of Jesus' burial clothes.

The fourth and fifth scenes in which the Beloved Disciple explicitly appears are also scenes in which Peter plays a prominent role. Both these scenes involve encounters with the risen Jesus, and John presents both of them in the final chapter of the Gospel.

In the following section of this study the three initiatives Peter takes during the fishing scene of chapter 21 will be considered in some detail. Peter acts consistently and with boldness throughout this scene. Nevertheless, the capacity of the Beloved Disciple to identify Jesus functions critically in this passage. He alone is able to point out that Jesus is the one directing them from the shore (21:7a): "It is the Lord." It is explicitly to Peter that the Beloved Disciple expresses this insight. For his part, Peter accepts the Beloved Disciple's identification of Jesus without a moment's hesitation, gathering his garments and diving immediately into the lake.[8]

As the scene unfolds, Peter, the Beloved Disciple, and the other five disciples in the boat reunite with Jesus on the beach. Note that this is now the fourth time that John has illuminated the Beloved Disciple's relationship with Jesus. At the Last Supper this disciple's close tie to Jesus and his status for speaking with Jesus were indicated. Chapter 19 showed Jesus entrusting his mother to this disciple's care. In chapter 20 his capacity for believing that Jesus has risen was portrayed. Now, at the beginning of chapter 21, this disciple's unique capability for recognizing the risen Jesus is profiled.

The final scene involving the Beloved Disciple is the final scene of the Gospel. Jesus and Peter have just interacted memorably on the shore of the Sea of Tiberias when Peter becomes concerned about the future of the Beloved Disciple:

> Peter turned and saw following them the disciple whom Jesus loved, who had lain close to his breast at the supper and had said, "Lord, who is it that is going to betray you?" When Peter saw him, he said to Jesus, "Lord, what about this man?" Jesus said to him, "If it is my will that he remain until I come, what is that to you? Follow me." (21:20-22)

The care with which John portrays the Beloved Disciple in this final scene is unmistakable. John's reintroduction of this disciple includes a verbatim rendering of the words this disciple spoke at the Last Supper. It is as though the evangelist wants his readers, especially his paradigmatic readers, to focus on the question of this disciple's future. What is the nature of Jesus' response regarding the future of this model disciple? The reply Jesus gives to Peter's question is enigmatic: "If it is my will that he *remain* until I come, what is that to you?" (21:22a; emphasis added).

Concluding reflections regarding the identity, calling, and destiny of the Beloved Disciple are now in order. The first two clauses[9] of 21:24 are extremely important for an interpretation of the identity of this disciple. They read: "This is the disciple who is bearing witness to these things, and who has written these things." These clauses imply that the Beloved Disciple is the principal author of the Gospel, a consideration that obviously possesses great significance for those reading his work.

In a similar way, the next verses also disclose the principal feature of this disciple's calling: his calling is no more and no less than that he *remain*. Jesus' words to Peter at 21:22 establish this, but at 21:23 the author (the Beloved Disciple himself) takes pains to clarify that this "remaining" does not mean that he is to be preserved from death. Until he dies, this "remaining with Jesus" is his principal calling. Nevertheless, the writing of the Gospel is now understood to be a principal fruit of this faithful disciple's dwelling with his Lord.

5. Peter during the Time of Jesus' Public Ministry[10]

As indicated in the preceding section, within John's Gospel Peter is the third disciple to follow Jesus. Andrew and an unnamed disciple (whom the evangelist may understand to be the Beloved Disciple) are the first in following. In the wake of his own encounter with Jesus, Andrew immediately seeks out his brother and thus becomes the intermediary by whom Peter comes to Jesus. In proclaiming to his brother "We have found the Messiah" (1:41b), Andrew is also the first disciple to identify Jesus as the Christ.

After Andrew brings Peter to him, Jesus responds in two ways. First he displays the superior knowledge he so frequently shows in John's Gospel: "So you are Simon, the son of John." (1:42b). Second, without any explanation of his reasons for this initiative, Jesus decisively changes Simon's name: "You shall be called Cephas." John subsequently explains that the name "Cephas" means "Peter" ("rock") but provides no additional explanation of the appropriateness of this name for Simon.[11]

As a brief elaboration, it should be noted that John's Gospel will henceforth employ three names for this disciple: "Simon Peter," "Peter," and "Simon."[12] A further feature to note in John's characterization of the first disciples is that, even though Peter is brought to Jesus through his brother's initiative, Andrew himself has already been introduced into the narrative at 1:40 as "Simon Peter's brother."

As observed in the preceding section, the Galilean crisis occurs in the wake of Jesus' proclamation that those who "eat me" will live "because of me" (6:57). John relates that many of Jesus' disciples drew back and ceased following him because of the "hardness" of this saying (6:60, 66). As analyzed above, it is at this juncture that Jesus questions the Twelve regarding their own intentions, and Peter responds boldly, affirming that he and the others will continue with undeviating faithfulness. Observe the use of the plural here; Peter is confidently venturing to speak on behalf of the other members of the Twelve: "Simon Peter answered him, 'Lord to whom shall we go? You have the words of eternal life; and we have believed, and have come to know, that you are the Holy One of God'" (6:68-69).

Peter's intervention here is noteworthy for the steadfast allegiance it expresses, but it is no less remarkable in its testimony to Jesus' exalted standing. Andrew earlier proclaimed Jesus' identity as the Christ. Peter now confesses the comparable truth that Jesus is "the Holy One of God." What is more, Peter also explicitly proclaims a salvific consequence of Jesus' exalted standing: Jesus provides "the words of eternal life."

It is useful to assess this passage in terms of the Johannine themes of "believing" and "remaining." Here Peter and the others have come to *believe* that Jesus is the Holy One of God and this belief grounds their unswerving allegiance. "Lord, to whom shall we go?" For Peter and those for whom he speaks there is *no one else* comparable to Jesus. And thus with Jesus they will *remain*.

Peter in John 13. Within this chapter John portrays Peter engaging in two remarkable conversations with Jesus. These conversations both occur within the framework of the Last Supper. Situated between these two conversations is the episode in which Peter asks the Beloved Disciple to learn from Jesus the identity of the betrayer.

It is useful to observe at the outset that, in different ways, Peter receives Jesus' affirmation at the end of both these conversations. What of Peter's performance during the course of these conversations? It will be seen that Peter is a mixture of bravado, faithfulness, misapprehension, and failure.

At 13:4-5, with the time of his departure at hand, Jesus, in a gesture of loving service, begins to wash his disciples' feet. When Jesus comes to Peter, this disciple tries to prevent any washing, exclaiming: "Lord, do you wash my feet?" (13:6b). Referencing the future, Jesus' initial response to Peter is, "What I am doing you do not know now, but afterwards you will understand" (13:7). Unmoved by Jesus' explanation, Peter replies emphatically: "You shall never wash my feet" (13:8a).

How is Peter being portrayed at this point? Does the evangelist not image him with a certain resoluteness that is reminiscent of the firmness he displayed in indicating his commitment to Jesus at 6:68? Nevertheless, as Jesus' next words make clear, Peter is not apprehending the deeper meaning Jesus intends, and which posits a link between Jesus' love in giving his life for his friends and the self-giving love expressed in this footwashing.

In focusing only on the footwashing Peter neglects this deeper dimension. In rejecting the footwashing he is implicitly, if unknowingly, separating himself from Jesus' giving of his life. Without explaining every aspect of this meaning, Jesus nevertheless confronts Peter with the truth that he will be separating himself from Jesus unless he consents to have his feet washed. Jesus' decisive words are: "If I do not wash you, you have no part in me" (13:8b).

Peter's own bold response, once he has grasped something of the meaning and the import Jesus attaches to this action, is: "Lord, not my feet only but also my hands and my head!" (13:9). In effect, then, Peter's revised position, expressed with boldness, reaffirms his desire to remain completely with Jesus. Jesus' own affirmation of Peter's renewed allegiance is expressed both by his next words about the general cleanness of the disciples (Peter included, but not the betrayer) and by the fact that Jesus then proceeds with the footwashing (13:10-12a).

The knowledge of coming betrayal that the evangelist attributes to Jesus at 13:11 is subsequently expressly articulated at 13:21. It is then that Peter, wanting to learn the betrayer's identity, asks the Beloved Disciple to inquire of Jesus. In reporting this initiative by Peter, what does the evangelist communicate regarding the relationship that exists between Peter and the Beloved Disciple?

The Beloved Disciple appears in the narrative for the first time in this passage, yet evidently this disciple (along with Peter and other named and unnamed disciples) has been following Jesus for some time. Peter seemingly respects this disciple as someone to whom Jesus will disclose such sensitive information. Further, Peter seemingly judges that the Beloved Disciple has such a respect for Peter that he will (a) agree to question Jesus as Peter wishes and (b) disclose to Peter the answer Jesus gives him.

Note also the forms of deference that are indicated here. In contrast with his pattern of addressing Jesus forthrightly at 6:68 and 13:6-9, Peter here does not attempt to address Jesus. Rather, he circumspectly speaks to the Beloved Disciple. In his turn the Beloved Disciple himself defers to Peter by carrying Peter's request forward to Jesus. Is there not in this entire scene a presentiment of the mutual respect and deference that the Beloved Disciple and Peter are more explicitly shown to practice when they interact at Jesus' tomb (20:3-10) and while fishing together on the Sea of Galilee (21:2-7)? However, as noted previously, John does not indicate whether the Beloved Disciple, in his turn, actually communicated Judas' identity to Peter.

Peter's second conversation with Jesus is precipitated by Jesus' words at 13:33b concerning his departure. With the directness he has twice previously exhibited (6:68 and 13:6-9), Peter asks Jesus (13:36): "Lord, where are you going?" Jesus' reply to Peter pertains to the present and the future. The future dimension in this answer is especially important. Nevertheless, Jesus' emphasis on Peter's inability to follow him at the present time is also significant. To highlight the contrast Jesus posits between Peter's present performance and his performance in the future, both dimensions of Peter's following will be italicized in the verse now to be cited: "Jesus answered, 'Where I am going you *cannot follow now*; but you *shall follow afterward*'" (13:36b). In effect Jesus' reply contains elements of both internal and external predictive prolepsis.

Jesus' sovereign knowledge regarding both dimensions of Peter's following is crucial for the interpretation of the passage and also for understanding the risen Jesus' words to Peter about "following" in 21:22. In John's narrative, 13:38 demonstrates that Jesus already knows that Peter will deny him three times. That is why Peter cannot follow Jesus now. In the testing that will occur within just a few hours Peter will not have the courage to keep following Jesus. Nevertheless, Jesus is already looking beyond Peter's present abject failure to a time when Peter will have the resoluteness for steadfast following.

Given the knowledge he consistently attributes to Jesus, the evangelist surely recognizes that it is ludicrous for Peter to try to set aside Jesus' warning about failure in the present. Nevertheless, he shows Peter pressing forward with the bold claim: "I will lay down my life for you" (13:37b). In the words Jesus speaks in reply, is there an aspect of irony over Peter's bravado mixed with an aspect of sadness but also with promise for the future? For Peter, are not Jesus' words akin to a stake driving into Peter's heart? How stark the unvarnished truth that, within hours, Peter will actually deny Jesus not once but three times! Once Jesus has delivered this shattering prediction, is it possible for Peter to hear, in a meaningful way, the words regarding faithful *future* following that Jesus has also just spoken?

Although Peter may not be able to respond to Jesus' words about his future, their importance in terms of John's unfolding narrative can scarcely be overstated. Let Jesus' words, "*but you shall follow afterward*" (19:36a), thus be magnified and positioned prominently as the background context for the devastating verbal exchange in which Peter's bravado is decisively punctured by Jesus.

> Peter said to him, "Lord, why cannot I follow you now? I will lay down my life for you." Jesus answered, "Will you lay down your life for me? Truly, truly, I say to you, the cock will not crow till you have denied me three times." (13:37-38)

Is Peter fully convinced by Jesus' words? John records no reply by Peter to this stunning prediction by Jesus. And Peter is not heard from throughout the remainder of the supper. Were it not for the fact that Peter's bold words are so quickly undermined by Jesus' prediction, Peter's declaration could be thought to express the zenith in his following of Jesus. How would John have his paradigmatic readers interpret Peter's subsequent silence? Has Peter imbibed Jesus' prediction to the degree that he recognizes the foolhardiness of the words he has just spoken? Or does Peter quietly reject Jesus' prediction and still cling to the conviction that he will be able to offer his life on Jesus' behalf?

Peter as Hireling in John 18. In John 18, Peter's behavior in the courtyard during Jesus' interrogation contrasts sharply with his actions in the garden during Jesus' arrest. In both scenes Peter's behavior intensely reflects his attitude toward Jesus. At first he is boldly defending Jesus; later he is virtually fleeing from all association with him.

For paradigmatic readers who read John 18 in the light of John 10, striking correlations emerge. In the garden Jesus (the good shepherd of 10:11, 14) refuses to let Judas, the officers of the high priest, and the soldiers (the thieves and robbers of 10:8) harm ("snatch" as in 10:29b) his disciples (the sheep who know the good shepherd as in 10:14).

Jesus' role and sovereignty as the Good Shepherd is also the key to Jesus' rebuke of Peter for striking with the sword. Because he is not mindful of Jesus' words that no one will take his life from him (10:14a), Peter uses his sword on Jesus' behalf. This deed evidences Peter's deep attachment to Jesus but also discloses that Peter has failed to grasp the true nature of Jesus' sovereignty and the character of Jesus' mission. Jesus' response to Peter's action again testifies to his sovereign power and his adherence to the plan according to which he has been sent (18:11): "Put your sword into its sheath; shall I not drink the cup which the Father has given me?"

In John's rendering of this scene Peter does not reply verbally to Jesus' rebuke. Peter's nonverbal response is, however, to *follow* Jesus to the high priest's courtyard. Given the standards of discipleship in John's Gospel, this is laudable behavior on Peter's part. Then, however, Peter's denials commence.

Especially for paradigmatic readers, John's report of the circumstances and character of Peter's first denial (18:17-18) contains four important details. First, there is a spatial similarity between the "courtyard" where Peter makes his denials and the "sheepfold" in which the good shepherd keeps his sheep: John 10:16 and 18:18 both image an enclosed space accessible through a guarded gate. (In the original Greek the evangelist has used the same word for both enclosures.) Second, there is the forceful character of Peter's denial. Peter attaches the negative modifier to two words Jesus has previously used to identify himself, thereby denying his Lord with the words "I am *not*."

Third, John shows Peter making this denial as he stands with the high priest's "officers" or "attendants," the same officers with whom Judas had stood in orchestrating Jesus' arrest. The fourth detail is the fact that Peter voices his denial to a group gathered around a charcoal fire. As John's narrative unfolds it will become clear to John's paradigmatic readers that there is an important link between this fire and the charcoal fire around which the risen Jesus gathers his disciples in John 21.

In John's account the first hostile question to Peter and his denial (18:17) are contrasted with the high priest's hostile question to Jesus and Jesus' faithful testimony (18:19-23). As a consequence of his testimony before Annas, Jesus is now sent *in bonds* (a more formal indication of his coming condemnation) to Caiaphas and then to Pilate (18:28). In effect, Jesus is moving forward with the laying down of his life, about which he had spoken earlier in John 10. At the time of his arrest Jesus the Good Shepherd provided for the safety of his sheep. Now Jesus the Good Shepherd moves forward to lay down his life for his flock.

John then shifts his spotlight back to Peter for the second part of Peter's own "trial" (18:25-27). Peter is in the same space, the same courtyard/sheepfold where Jesus is located. In contrast with Jesus, who is consciously proceeding forward with the laying down of his life, Peter's denials reflect a fear that he will lose his life. In stark contrast to his vow at 13:37 that he will lay down his life for Jesus, Peter now proceeds to deny any association with Jesus. In an attempt to preserve his life, Peter elects to flee from *the good shepherd* just as the hireling flees from *the good shepherd's* sheep when he sees danger approaching (10:12).[13]

Peter's second denial is made with precisely the same words as his first: "I am not" (18:25c). The third denial comes in response to a query from a relative of Malchus, insinuating that Peter was "with him" (Jesus) in the garden (18:26). In now recalling Peter's severance of Malchus' ear, does John suggest that Peter has a fear of retribution for this specific deed as well as a general concern for being harmed if he is identified as a disciple of Jesus? Peter is consciously fleeing from any identification with Jesus his shepherd. Nevertheless, he has ample reason to be afraid.

When Peter again denies that he is/was with Jesus, his fleeing from Jesus is complete and the cock crows to signal the fulfillment of his Lord's prediction (18:27). Just as there is no provision for the hireling of John 10 to express remorse for his flight from the sheep, so now there is no provision for the hireling of John 18 to express remorse for his abandonment of the Good Shepherd. Having denied Jesus the third time, Peter simply vanishes from John's narrative until after Jesus' resurrection.

What is Peter's standing at this point in comparison with Jesus' other disciples? By likening his behavior to that of a hireling who flees, John portrays Peter as the least of Jesus' disciples, apart from Judas, in terms of the criteria of following and remaining. One other of Jesus' friends, perhaps the Beloved Disciple, has followed Jesus to the high priest's courtyard. Absent mention to the contrary, this disciple presumably continues to follow Jesus. Certainly the Beloved Disciple follows Jesus for the duration: John explicitly portrays him in physical proximity to Jesus' cross.

If the Beloved Disciple's faithful *following* far surpasses Peter's *fleeing*, what of Jesus' other disciples? While they do not emulate the Beloved Disciple in his following and remaining, neither do they emulate Peter is his fleeing. When Jesus provides for their escape at 18:8 they are effectively shielded from the decision whether to follow or flee. It thus emerges that Peter is in a class by himself. Recognizing his brave intentions and his initial following and accepting that he has grounds for his fears, he is still the only one of Jesus' disciples to flee!

6. Peter and the Risen Jesus

Given the complexity of John's portrayal of the risen Jesus and Peter in John 21, it is useful to treat that chapter as a specific subsection after the treatment of John 20 has been completed.

A. *Peter in John 20*

The joint visit by the Beloved Disciple and Peter to Jesus' tomb in John 20 has been discussed in section four above. After the two disciples depart from the tomb, the risen Jesus manifests himself to Mary Magdalene and commissions her to announce his ascending to the Father (20:11-17). Obedient to this commission, Mary then proceeds "to the disciples" (unnamed) and tells them of her encounter with the Lord (20:18).

On the evening of that same day Jesus miraculously appears to "the disciples," commissioning them for the forgiving and retaining of sins (external predictive prolepsis) and entrusting the Holy Spirit to them (20:19-23). Although he remarks that these disciples were glad to see their risen Lord, John does not name any of those gathered except Thomas, who is identified because of his absence and his initial unbelief. Eight days later "his disciples" are gathered in the same location (20:26). In this instance Thomas is present in the group and becomes the focus of Jesus' attention (20:27-29). Thomas' solemn acclamation of Jesus as "my Lord and my God" then closes this chapter in such a way as to echo the exalted statement regarding Jesus' standing given in the very first verse of the Gospel.

But what of Peter's own belief in Jesus? What of his specific remorse for having behaved as a hireling during his own "trial" in the high priest's courtyard? Chapter 20 has said relatively little about the relationship between the risen Jesus and Peter. For John's paradigmatic readers this represents a relative "gap" in the narrative that will be filled abundantly in John 21.

B. *Peter and the Risen Jesus in John 21*

Given the complex subtleties of John 21's links with the body of the Gospel and given the astonishing initiatives this chapter attributes to Jesus on behalf of Peter, it is useful to provide a few overview comments at the very outset. The narrative of the chapter divides into two principal segments: The first concerns the disciples' miraculous catch of fish and their encounter with Jesus on the shore of the lake. The second contains an intensely personal conversation between Jesus and Peter after the lakeside breakfast. This conversation further divides into two parts: (a) Jesus' rehabilitation and commissioning of Peter for pastoral ministry and (b) Jesus' commissioning of Peter for the role of martyr.

As they approach his 21st chapter, John's paradigmatic readers are sensitive to the fact that nothing in John 20 addressed the phenomenon of Peter's behavior as a hireling in John 18. They are also sensitive to the fact that Jesus' prediction for Peter at 13:36b (". . . but you shall follow afterward") has not yet been fulfilled. These paradigmatic readers, as well as John's less acute readers, will find that in addition to addressing Peter's earlier failure to remain with the Good Shepherd, John 21 actually entrusts Peter with the role of caring for the Good Shepherd's sheep. This is the great irony the readers of John 21 now encounter: Peter, who earlier fled like a hireling from the Good Shepherd's side, is now commissioned by the Shepherd to feed and care for his sheep.

In the narrative of John 21 Peter's occupation is identified for the first time. John now indicates that he is versed in fishing; possibly he is the owner of a boat and nets. At the same time that Peter's experience with fishing is signaled, John also portrays him as someone whose lead the other disciples follow. When he announces: "I am going fishing" (21:3), the other disciples reply: "We will go with you." The following disciples take their places in the boat: Simon Peter first, then Thomas, Nathanael, the sons of Zebedee, and two other unnamed disciples. It will subsequently emerge that the Beloved Disciple is one of those in the boat.

Jesus' appearance on the beach opens a new sequence of events, in which Peter is portrayed favorably in at least six ways. First, Peter and all the others in the boat accept the mysterious stranger's directive regarding a better way to fish (21:6). Second, the Beloved Disciple, whose role in identifying Jesus as the stranger on the shore is pivotal, speaks his insight directly to Peter (21:7a). Third, Peter's response reflects a desire to get to Jesus immediately: he tucks in his garment and springs into the sea to do so (21:7b). Fourth, Peter hastens to do Jesus' bidding to bring some of the fish they have just caught. Spontaneously and without assistance he hauls ashore the net full of large fish.

Before we proceed to list other facets of John 21's favorable portrayal of Peter, it is appropriate to reflect that, because of Jesus' initiative, Peter has now fished with great success. The catch Peter and the others have made is so bounteous that the entire group of disciples is not able to haul in the net (21:6). Yet Peter responds to Jesus' subsequent directive and singlehandedly hauls ashore a net that contains 153 large fish (21:11a). Further, he does so without tearing the net (21:11b). Do these literal and symbolic features indicate John's view that Jesus is preparing Peter, as well as the other disciples, to evangelize and to keep the expanding community of disciples unified?

As John proceeds with his description of the lakeside scene, his reference to the charcoal fire Jesus uses to prepare fish and bread (21:9) brings this scene together with the earlier courtyard scene in which Peter emphatically denied being Jesus' disciple. In that previous scene Peter faced a threefold interrogation *about Jesus*. Now he faces a threefold interrogation *by Jesus*.[14] In both cases it is Peter's *relationship* to Jesus that is at issue.

The fifth positive facet in John 21's portrayal of Peter is the profession of love he gives in response to each of Jesus' three queries. There are similarities in the three questions.[15] In each Jesus solemnly addresses Peter as "Simon, son of John," the form of address he used at 1:42 in first calling him. Also, each question focuses on the issue of Peter's love for Jesus. It is the first question that tests Peter the most, for in it Jesus not only asks if Peter loves him; he also asks if Peter loves him "more than these" (21:15b).

What is the meaning of these words? Are they intended to ascertain whether Peter loves Jesus more than he loves his fishing companions? Are they meant to determine whether Peter loves Jesus more than the boat and the net, the other fishing appurtenances he has just been using? Given the Johannine Peter's previous penchant for exaggerated claims that tend to set him apart from Jesus' other disciples,[16] the best interpretation is that these words invite Peter to claim that he personally loves Jesus better than any of the other disciples do.

If Jesus' first question is thus designed to test Peter's humility and modesty, Peter passes this test exemplarily. His response eschews any comparisons, any setting of himself apart from the others in their respective love for Jesus. Peter replies only: "Yes, Lord; you know that I love you" (21:15b). Jesus' second question does not invite Peter to enter into comparisons, but simply asks again regarding his own love. Peter replies just as he did to the first question: Jesus is his Lord and Jesus knows that Peter loves him.

The hurt and the ardor Peter expresses in his reply to Jesus' third question mark a sixth way in which he is favorably profiled in this section of the Gospel. The evangelist writes that it "grieved" Peter (21:17b) that he had to be asked a third time. Nevertheless, he unhesitatingly states his love for Jesus once again, adding poignantly that Jesus himself already knows the truth of Peter's words because Jesus "knows all things" (21:17c).

This interpretation of John 21 has thus far established Peter's emergence as a fisherman whom Jesus directs to an almost inconceivably rich catch of fish. It has also been established that Peter's three affirmations of his love enable him to "overcome" his three denials of Jesus reported in John 18. It now remains to consider the two commissions Jesus entrusts to Peter in conjunction with his three professions of love. These two "commissions" both represent instances of external predictive prolepsis.

Up to this point the analysis of the three interactions between Jesus and Peter has focused on Jesus' questions to Peter and Peter's responses. Now attention must be given to the commissions Jesus gives to Peter after each of Peter's replies. Just as Jesus' three questions to Peter were fundamentally the same and Peter's three replies were fundamentally the same, so is there a basic similarity in these three commissions: "Feed my lambs" (21:15c); "Tend my sheep" (21:16c); "Feed my sheep" (21:17c).

What is the precise nature of Peter's new role? It is to feed and tend the sheep that belong to Jesus. Earlier in the Gospel Jesus has emphasized his own role in caring for his sheep, imaging himself as the Good Shepherd. Now he is entrusting the care of his sheep to Peter. In principle the specific concerns Jesus expressed in John 10 relative to his sheep all transfer to Peter under his new mandate for tending and feeding Jesus' sheep. These include the future-oriented ministries that Jesus' words at 10:16 identify: "And I have other sheep that are not of this fold. I must bring them also, and they will heed my voice. So there shall be one flock, one shepherd."

What has Peter done to warrant such an auspicious commission? Given what has been disclosed in John's preceding narrative, this commission is fully unmerited. In the decisive events of Jesus' trial and crucifixion Peter has shown himself to be a hireling. Nevertheless, Jesus' questions to Peter give him the opportunity to profess his love for the Good Shepherd. And as Peter does so, the Good Shepherd freely elects to select him for the care of the Good Shepherd's sheep! John 21 portrays this initiative as belonging solely to Jesus, just as John 1 showed the initiative belonging solely to Jesus when he gave Simon the name of Peter and called him into discipleship.

In John 10 the hallmark that identifies and establishes Jesus as the Good Shepherd is his willingness to lay down his life for his sheep (10:11, 15, 17, 18). This is what distinguishes him from the hireling. Yet in John 18 Peter became the hireling. How will he now become a shepherd in the manner of Jesus? Peter's deep love for the Good Shepherd is one way in which he becomes "qualified" for this new role.

It remains for Peter to become qualified for pastoring Jesus' sheep by reason of his willingness to lay down his life. And Jesus points Peter toward this further means of qualification in 21:18-19. Indeed, Jesus' words and the evangelist's clarifying note, taken together, indicate that Roman crucifixion will be the precise means through which Peter lays down his life:

> Truly, truly, I say to you, when you were young, you girded yourself and walked where you would; but when you are old, you will stretch out your hands, and another will gird you and carry you where you do not wish to go." (This he said to show by what death he was to glorify God.) And after this he said to him, "Follow me." (John 21:18-19)

In effect Peter, just commissioned to shepherd Jesus' sheep, is now also commissioned to enter upon the same form of death by which Jesus gave his life. These two aspects, the pastoring of Jesus' sheep and the laying down of his life in the mode of Jesus, are linked. Only Jesus' earlier prediction that some of his disciples will experience death at the hands of the political authorities (16:2b)[17] prepares John's paradigmatic readers for this new prediction that Peter himself will specifically suffer crucifixion.

In the final verse of the passage just cited Jesus renews his previous call that Peter *follow* him.[18] This renewed invitation for Peter to follow links with Jesus' earlier words to Peter when he said (a) that Peter could not follow him *now* and (b) that Peter would follow him *afterwards* (13:36). Just as the prediction that Peter would not follow Jesus "now" was fulfilled through Peter's three denials, Jesus' promise that Peter will follow him "afterwards" is now specified in the prediction that Peter will follow him in undergoing crucifixion.

One segment of Jesus' lakeshore conversation with Peter remains to be considered. Peter's next question suggests that he is now no longer beset by his former fear of crucifixion, a compelling fear that led him to his three denials. He now speaks to Jesus with equanimity and ease, not anxious regarding his own looming future but, rather, curious regarding the Beloved Disciple's future. As the following excerpt indicates, Jesus answers Peter's inappropriate question and then admonishes Peter not to be concerned about the Beloved Disciple's path, but rather to keep focused on the demands of his own "following."

> Peter turned and saw following them the disciple whom Jesus loved, who had lain close to his breast at the supper and had said, "Lord, who is it that is going to betray you?" When Peter saw him, he said to Jesus, "Lord, what about this man? Jesus said to him, "If it is my will that he remain until I come, what is that to you? Follow me!" The saying spread abroad among the brethren that this disciple was not to die; yet Jesus did not say to him that he was not to die, but, "If it is my will that he remain until I come, what is that to you?" (21:20-23)

Is it not the sense of John's narrative that a remarkable familiarity and ease characterizes Peter's relationship with Jesus at this point? Peter has performed well in immediately diving into the water to get to Jesus' side, in hauling ashore the large net filled with fish, and in affirming three times that he loves Jesus. He has then received an extraordinary pastoral commission from Jesus, and he now receives the promise that, as Jesus' martyr, he will undergo the same form of execution Jesus himself underwent. Emboldened by the aura of reconciliation and intimacy that pervades this entire encounter, Peter now boldly asks about the fate of the Beloved Disciple.

In this, Peter moves beyond the bounds of propriety. Accordingly, Jesus admonishes him that the particular future Jesus will entrust to the Beloved Disciple is not Peter's business! In addition, Jesus also admonishes Peter to concentrate on what is involved in his own future following of Jesus. Jesus' renewed command for Peter to follow him features the same Greek verb as at 21:19, but this time the personal pronoun is employed for the sake of emphasis. The firmness with which Jesus speaks to Peter at 21:22b has been notably rendered into English in the translation proposed by a contemporary commentator (italics in original):[19] "As for you, *you follow me*."

6. Summary of Peter's Portrayal in John

After Jesus calls him (Andrew, his brother, having been called first) and renames him, Peter's major contribution before the Last Supper is to declare his allegiance to Jesus as the Holy One of God, precisely at the time when other disciples are leaving in shock over Jesus' teachings. At the Last Supper, after initially rejecting Jesus' proposal to wash his feet, Peter then accepts it and even affirms that his allegiance to Jesus will be unto death.

Peter's subsequent sword blow defending Jesus and his effort to follow him both express the allegiance he has just professed. Nevertheless, when challenged in the courtyard Peter vehemently denies Jesus three times, in effect playing the role of a hireling who abandons the Good Shepherd at the time of danger. Peter's failure at this point is underscored by the contrast the evangelist draws between his behavior and the unwavering faithfulness manifested by the Beloved Disciple.

Nevertheless, John's unfolding account discloses that the risen Jesus desires to restore Peter and to commission him for new ministries. At the tomb Peter does not yet believe, but he is brought to belief by Jesus' Easter evening appearance to the assembled group of disciples. Subsequently, in the narrative of John 21, Peter conforms fully to Jesus' instructions for fishing and three times avows his personal love for Jesus. Jesus then entrusts this erstwhile "hireling" with the care of Jesus' sheep and predicts that Peter's future will involve death by crucifixion.

Summary of Peter's Trajectory and Predicted Future in John

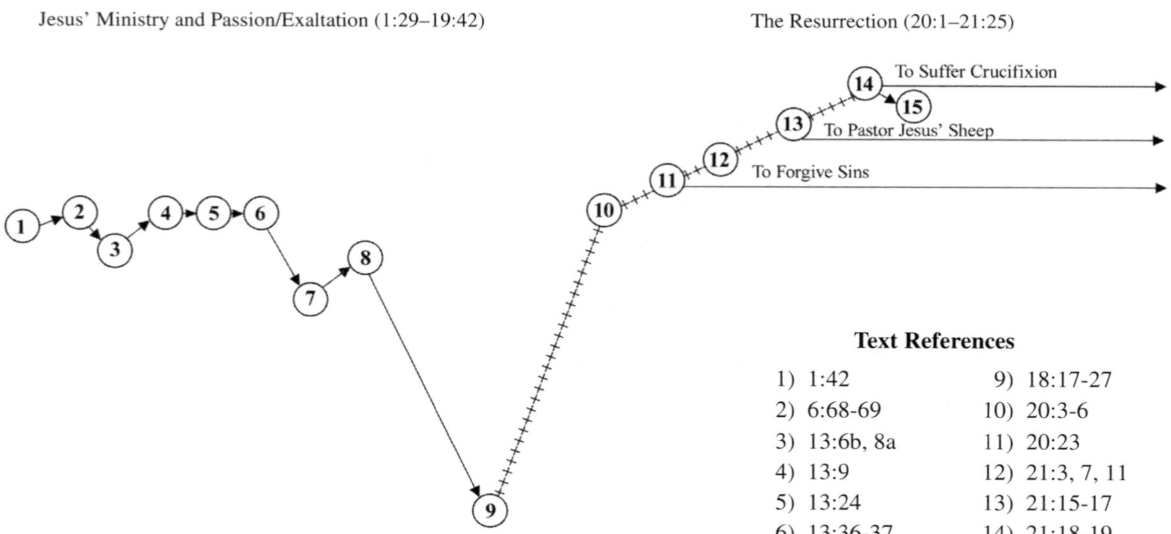

Text References

1) 1:42	9) 18:17-27
2) 6:68-69	10) 20:3-6
3) 13:6b, 8a	11) 20:23
4) 13:9	12) 21:3, 7, 11
5) 13:24	13) 21:15-17
6) 13:36-37	14) 21:18-19
7) 18:10	15) 21:21-22
8) 18:15-16	

+ + + + Emphasizes Jesus' Sovereign Intervention

CHAPTER SIX

The Reception of the Four Gospels at Philippi

This chapter will present an analysis of various social, political, and religious factors at Philippi in order to suggest some of the ways each Gospel's portrayal of Peter might have been received by Christian readers at Philippi. The final section of this chapter will then offer some concluding reflections concerning the reception of these Gospel portrayals at other locations beyond Philippi.

Why have I selected Philippi as a test case? Two important considerations are: (a) The Christian community at Philippi is Pauline in origin, and (b) by reason of their location in a Roman colony the members of this community can be presumed to be particularly sensitive to John's image of "the crucified Peter." A further consideration is the high probability that Philippi was not a site at which any of the canonical Gospels was written.

1. Philippi and the Christian Community at Philippi

The following paragraphs offer only a broad-stroke presentation of Philippi's economic, social, and political context. Similarly, only a very general description will be given of the Christian community there. Lacunae may well exist in what is presented in this regard. Nevertheless, my intention is that what is presented provide a sufficient basis for informed conjecture.

A. *Philippi's Character and Its Status as a Roman Colony*[1]

Two principal economic factors contributed to Philippi's development in the first century C.E. The first was its strategic location on the Via Egnatia, the main road from Rome to its easternmost European provinces. The second was the high agricultural value of the land in the fertile plain in which the city was located. In addition to these economic factors, a principal political factor contributing to Philippi's development was its official designation as a Roman "colony."

While Philippi existed for centuries before the Roman empire (the city actually acquired its name as a consequence of being protected by Philip II of Macedonia in the fourth century B.C.E.), its designation as an official Roman "colony" came after Octavian (later to rule as "Augustus") and Mark Antony defeated the forces of Brutus and Cassius at Philippi in 42 B.C.E. Augustus further enhanced Philippi's standing as a colony after he defeated Antony at Actium in 31 B.C.E. In both instances the victorious general was concerned to provide well for the legionaries under his command.

To this end, these supreme Roman leaders determined that those serving in the legions would receive Roman citizenship and, upon their retirement after twenty-five years of service, a significant grant of land. On the one hand these benefits were a mechanism for solidifying the allegiance of those legionaries who had not yet reached the age of retirement. On the other hand, having settlements of highly trained veterans along its frontiers provided for the security of the empire in areas where it was not feasible to deploy Roman legions.

Once Philippi was officially designated a colony, it became an approved site for such grants of lands and gained a significant number of Roman veterans. By some estimates as many as two or three thousand veterans relocated to Philippi.[2] In becoming a colony Philippi received other forms of legal and tax privileges as well. Arguably, when Paul arrived there around 49 C.E.[3] Philippi was one of the most highly Romanized cities outside Italy.[4] A quarter or more of its population may have been Roman citizens; further, the members of this segment of the population exercised influence far beyond their numbers due to the status that accrued to them as veterans and holders of valuable land.[5]

Given the focus of the present study, it is useful to adduce two corollaries from what has just been said about Philippi's Roman veterans and its character as a Roman colony. The first concerns the presence of the *cursus honorum*, "the course of honors," at Philippi. This social system for achieving status and honor was dominant in Rome itself and was present outside Rome especially within the Roman legions and Roman colonies.

The second corollary concerns the Philippians' familiarity with the practice of crucifixion. It is reasonable to conjecture that Roman veterans and their descendants settled at Philippi had more than casual acquaintance with this signature form of Roman execution. Even veterans who had not witnessed the enactment of crucifixion almost certainly possessed a basic appreciation for the degradation and intimidation the Roman authorities intended when they crucified various types of "troublemakers."

B. *The Christian Community at Philippi*

What salient features of the Christian community at Philippi can we identify? In a previous study I have analyzed Paul's letter to the Philippians for clues about the character of the community to whom he was writing. His letter, very probably written from Rome in the early to mid-60s, reflects a primarily Gentile readership, something that is corroborated by Luke's description in Acts 16 of Paul's founding of this community.

A corollary flowing from the community's Gentile Christian character is that the majority of its members did not have an inherent familiarity with the Jewish context of Jesus' ministry in Galilee and Judea. How much information did the Philippian Christians possess about Jesus' earthly ministry and the role played by his first disciples? A precise answer cannot be given to this question. Nor can a precise answer be given to the specific question of how much information the Philippian Christians had about Peter.

Presumably, much of what the Philippian Christians initially learned about these topics came to them from Paul. Still, given the complex ways in which the Christian movement spread, including written and oral interactions among various Christian communities, very little can be said with certainty as to what the Christian community at Philippi knew about these topics before the first written Gospel arrived there.

Because of the community's location in a highly Romanized context and because numerous members of the community were Roman veterans or family members of veterans, what was said above regarding familiarity with the *cursus honorum* and with crucifixion is relevant at this point. Paul's reference in Philippians to Jesus' voluntary embrace of suffering and death, "even death on a cross" (2:8c), speaks powerfully of a "course of shame" that is in stark contrast to the "course of honor." Further, Paul's intimation that he himself may be "poured as a libation" (2:17a) and his reflection that he now faces the possibility of "becoming like him [Jesus] in his death" (3:10c) both have the capacity to resonate powerfully for readers and hearers who know well the meaning of a Roman death decree.

Finally, a word must be said about the capacity of the Christians at Philippi for embarking on a sophisticated reading of the texts of the four Gospels. Is it reasonable to posit that "paradigmatic reading" took place within this community? Recall that paradigmatic readers have the willingness to read and re-read the text of a Gospel in such a way that they grasp the light that the ending of the narrative sheds on all that has preceded. Further, paradigmatic readers have the capacity to identify each evangelist's subtle use of such elements as structure, plot, time, and setting.

It is only possible to conjecture the answer to this question. How many of the Christians at Philippi were literate? Of those who were literate, how many had the sophistication necessary for this type of reading? Two considerations argue for the presence of paradigmatic reading at Philippi. The first is the assumption that disciples of Jesus thirsted for information about him and all aspects of his earthly mission. Thus when any Gospel arrived at Philippi it presumably became subject to *multiple* re-readings. As those reading and hearing repeatedly entered into each evangelist's narrative, is it not probable that details that might have escaped their notice during their initial readings eventually came to be recognized as the reading process continued?

The second assumption concerns Philippi's place within the network of Christian communities. Each Gospel came not only to Philippi, but also to various other Christian locations within the empire. It is thus reasonable to conceive that, over the course of time, reading insights from the various Christian communities would be shared.[6] In effect, then, if paradigmatic readers were lacking at Philippi there is reason to hold that the insights from paradigmatic readers elsewhere would eventually reach Philippi.

2. Images of Peter from Paul's Writings

This section conjectures that, before the arrival of a Gospel at Philiippi, Paul himself and two of Paul's letters were the principal sources for the Philippian Christians' image of Peter. This conjecture itself rests on the supposition that 1 Corinthians and Galatians both reached Philippi before any Gospel. In order to keep Paul and his letters as the principal factor for consideration, I further suppose that the Acts of the Apostles did not arrive in Philippi until after the Gospels reached there. (This latter supposition is more tentative than the former.)

Certainly the Christians at Philippi could have learned about Peter from a variety of other sources in addition to Paul and his letters. For example, some members may have had personal contact with Peter within the unfolding Christian movement. Further oral and even written reports about Peter's role both during Jesus' ministry and subsequent to his resurrection might have been transmitted to Philippi from other Christian communities in a variety of ways. Nevertheless, while recognizing the potential influence of these and other sources, I choose to concentrate on 1 Corinthians and Galatians because they are *written texts* (and hence concretely accessible for study) from *the founder* of the community at Philippi.

First Corinthians and Galatians are the only letters in which Paul makes reference to Peter. In these letters Paul refers to this disciple as "Cephas" a total of eight times, but he does not say anything about the origin or meaning of this name. Further, Paul is aware of the Greek rendering of this disciple's name; he uses "Peter" twice in Galatians.

While the data they supply is not extensive, both letters do provide perspectives on Paul's estimation of Peter and Peter's role. The first broad perspective that emerges is that Paul regards Peter as a disciple/apostle of considerable standing. The second is that, according to Jesus' intention, Paul possesses a commission to apostleship that is not secondary to Peter's.

In I Corinthians Paul makes four references to "Cephas." In the first two of these references (1:12 and 3:21-22) he is striving to combat factions and writes to the Corinthian Christians to cease identifying themselves as belonging to Paul or Apollos or Cephas. In the third reference (9:5) Paul is defending his own standing as an apostle and comments that he has the same right to be accompanied by a wife as do "the other apostles and the brothers of the Lord and Cephas."

Paul's fourth reference in I Corinthians is significant both for the standing it attributes to Cephas and for the comparable standing Paul claims. Paul is testifying to the Resurrection of Jesus but he also indicates to the Corinthians that, because of the risen Lord's appearance to him, he has received the same confirmation received first by Cephas and subsequently by others. Further, Paul claims, by grace, to have worked more energetically:

> . . . that he was buried, that he was raised on the third day in accordance with the scriptures, and that he appeared to Cephas, then to the twelve. Then he appeared to more than five hundred brethren at one time, most of whom are still alive, though some have fallen asleep. Then he appeared to James, then to all the apostles. Last of all, as to one untimely born, he appeared also to me. For I am the least of the apostles, unfit to be called an apostle, because I persecuted the church of God. But by the grace of God I am what I am, and his grace toward me was not in vain. On the contrary, I worked harder than any of them, though it was not I, but the grace of God which is with me. (15:4-10).

Paul's references to Cephas in Galatians also reflect the two fundamental perspectives just identified. After initially stressing the "authorization" given him as a consequence of his encounter with the risen Jesus, Paul relates: "Then after three years I went up to Jerusalem to visit Cephas and remained with him fifteen days" (1:18). He adds that he did not confer with any of the other apostles except James, the Lord's brother.

In chapter 2 of Galatians Paul continues his defense against those questioning the soundness of his preaching and stresses especially the confirmation he received from the leaders of the Jerusalem church when he visited them after fourteen years. Within Galatians 2 there are two passages that mention Cephas. The first details Paul's experience at this second Jerusalem meeting, in which James, Cephas (note that Paul also uses the name "Peter" twice within this passage), and John were all prominent:

> . . . but on the contrary, when they saw that I had been entrusted with the gospel to the uncircumcised, just as Peter had been entrusted with the gospel to the circumcised (for he who worked through Peter for the mission to the circumcised worked through me also for the Gentiles), and when they perceived the grace that was given to me, James and Cephas and John, who were reputed to be pillars, gave to me and Barnabas the right hand of fellowship, that we should go to the Gentiles and they to the circumcised. . . . (2:7-9)

The next passage to be cited follows directly on Paul's account of this Jerusalem meeting. Since the setting is now Antioch, Paul presumes that the Galatians will discern that an interval of time has now elapsed. In this passage Paul details his public rebuke of Cephas. The dynamics of the situation to which Paul is referring are not completely explained (for example, Paul does not indicate how or whether Peter replied to Paul's criticism). Nevertheless, the central reality in the situation Paul describes is that Peter has deviated from the truth of the Gospel that Paul is authorized to proclaim:

> But when Cephas came to Antioch I opposed him to his face because he stood condemned. For before certain men came from James, he ate with the Gentiles; but when they came he drew back and separated himself, fearing the circumcision party. And with him the rest of the Jews acted insincerely, so that even Barnabas was carried away by their insincerity. But when I saw that they were not straightforward about the truth of the Gospel, I said to Cephas before them all, "If you, though a Jew, live like a Gentile and not like a Jew, how can you compel the Gentiles to live like Jews?" (2:11-14)

3. The Arrival of the Gospels at Philippi

The set of conjectures formulated in the preceding section will now be complemented by another set regarding the arrival of each Gospel at Philippi[7] and the reception of each Gospel's portrayal of Peter within that setting. The central conjecture of the preceding section has been that Paul's own written references to Peter exercised a significant influence on the image of Peter that the Philippian Christians had formed. The present section presumes the validity of that conjecture and seeks to relate "Peter according to Paul" with Peter according to each of the Gospels.

In what follows I especially invite each reader to assess the facets I identify in each Gospel as examples of what might have particular relevance for readers at Philippi. I will conjecture that the sheer gratuitousness of Peter's restorations by Jesus (Peter's "justification by grace") is a noteworthy feature of Mark's narrative. In Luke, Peter's standing as an apostle mandated to strengthen Jesus' other apostles is a significant aspect. Peter's commission to serve as a rock for Jesus' church is an important facet of Matthew's presentation. In John, Jesus' prediction that Peter will suffer Roman-enacted crucifixion is a portentous datum for the community at Roman-influenced Philippi.

A final preliminary note concerns the order in which the four Gospels will be treated in this section. I will adhere to the previous sequence of Mark, Luke, Matthew, and John. However, just as this study took no position regarding the order in which the Gospels were composed, it now takes no position regarding the order in which they actually arrived at Philippi. It should also be emphasized that, once a given Gospel arrived at Philippi, it inevitably modified the context in which the Philippians responded to the portrayal of Peter in any Gospel that arrived later.

A. *The Arrival of Mark's Gospel at Philippi*

In conjecturing the impact of Mark's portrayal of Peter at Philippi it is important to begin with reflections about the way in which paradigmatic readers and others might have responded to the first Gospel to reach them. In effect, readers of the present study are now invited to enter imaginatively into the reading experience of first-century paradigmatic readers in the Christian community at Philippi.

Suppose that, before the arrival of Mark's Gospel, the Christians at Philippi had been primarily formed through the Gospel that Paul preached and other oral reports about Jesus they had received from associates of Paul and others in the Christian movement. A written text now arrives in their city. Far from being merely a collection of Jesus' teachings and stories about him, this text is actually a *narrative*. Further, it is a narrative that provides a comprehensive overview of Jesus' public ministry including his suffering, death, and resurrection.

It is difficult to overemphasize the significance of the arrival of the first Gospel at Philippi. Did it come in codex or scroll form? Who brought it? What were the arrangements for this Gospel's first readings? Formulating questions such as these can help to engender a vicarious participation in the excitement that presumably attended the arrival of Mark's Gospel at Philippi.

The considerations about the role of paradigmatic readers that were listed in chapter 1 of this study now come to the fore. A decisive attribute of such readers is their willingness to enter upon multiple re-readings of the text with a view to uncovering its subtle connections and nuances. At Philippi such readers presumably began their readings by focusing on Mark's portrayal of Jesus, striving to grasp every datum and facet of this Gospel regarding their Lord. Yet even in their first readings of Mark's narrative these readers could not have avoided some preliminary engagement with the portrait Mark was also painting of Peter.

Their subsequent readings of the Gospel presumably disclosed still other subtle facets of the way in which Peter functions in terms of Jesus' mission. Over time, the full nuances of Mark's portrayal of Peter, as it is summarized in the paragraphs below, would have gradually become apparent to them. Finally, as they entered intensely into the process of reading Mark's account, they presumably reflected on what they were now learning about Peter within the framework of what they had previously learned of him from Paul.

In Mark, Peter (Simon) is the first disciple Jesus calls, and he calls him to be a "fisher of human beings" (1:16-18). Jesus then subsequently visits Simon's house and cures his mother-in-law (1:29-31). When Jesus later calls him to be a member of the Twelve, Simon's foremost responsibility is "to be with him" (3:14-16). On this occasion Jesus also changes this disciple's name from Simon to "Peter" (3:16).

As Mark's narrative unfolds, Peter emerges as a member of Jesus' inner circle, but the performance of all the disciples, Peter included, in understanding Jesus' identity and mission is seriously limited for most of the remainder of Part I of the Gospel. At the very end of this section Peter dramatically confesses Jesus' identity as the Christ (8:27-30), yet only verses later Peter plummets downward when he tries to dissuade Jesus from the path of suffering and gains Jesus' rebuke for being an agent of Satan! (8:32-33). Then, in a facet of the narrative that is difficult to assimilate unless Jesus' decisive sovereignty is grasped, Jesus acts to renew Peter's discipleship by inviting him to witness Jesus' transfiguration (9:2-8).

The performance of the disciples as a group, Peter included, deteriorates in Part II of the Gospel as they continue to misapprehend and reject Jesus' predictions regarding suffering, service, and the cross. At the Last Supper, when Jesus predicts that they will all forsake him, Peter boldly protests that he will not fall away (14:29) and then, trying to discount Jesus' predictions of his own denials, Peter states (14:31): "If I must die with you, I will not deny you."

Nevertheless, as the Passion begins, Peter first sleeps (14:37-41) and then flees (14:50). He recovers to try to be with Jesus, but after reaching the high priest's courtyard he egregiously denies Jesus three times (14:66-71). At this point the evangelist credits him with severe anguish (14:72), but Peter never does reach the cross "with Jesus." He has abjectly failed in his discipleship. What will happen to him now?

When Christians who are reading Mark's Gospel at Philippi (especially those who are paradigmatic readers) reach its conclusion, they discover that Peter's separation from Jesus is not allowed to stand! Previously in the narrative Jesus had predicted to his disciples that, after he was raised, he would go before them to Galilee (14:28), and at 16:7 this is what the angel instructs the faithful women to communicate: "But go tell his disciples and Peter that he is going before you to Galilee; there you will see him as he told you."

This, then, is the concluding image the Philippian Christians take with them from Mark's Gospel: Jesus sovereignly intervening to restore Peter to relationship with him. Earlier in the Gospel Jesus had accomplished a foreshadowing of this restoration when, by inviting Peter's presence for the Transfiguration, he brought him back from the position of rejecting Jesus' suffering and thereby serving as an agent of Satan. Now Peter is brought back from the tearful, dreadful isolation he had brought on himself through his denials of Jesus.

It must be emphasized that the degree to which the Christians at Philippi have embraced Paul's own story and his proclamation of "the Gospel of grace," is the degree to which they will resonate with the story of sheer grace that is at the heart of Mark's portrayal of Peter. Mark offers the Philippians no specifics as to any mission Peter might receive in the future except for two external predictive prolepses. The first is simply that Peter will be "with Jesus." The second is that he will face persecution.

The austere but fundamental truth to be drawn from the conclusion of Mark's Gospel is that Peter receives from Jesus a completely "unjustified" restoration to the status of being with him. Peter, who had egregiously separated himself from Jesus, is now entrusted with a future discipleship only for this reason: that Jesus, who chose him at the beginning, now, according to his own sovereign purposes, chooses him once again.

B. *The Arrival of Luke's Gospel at Philippi*

In their reading and hearing of Luke's Gospel the Christians of Philippi first encounter Peter when Jesus goes to Simon's house and cures his mother-in-law. They then meet him in vivid detail when Jesus formally calls him into ministry.

In response to Jesus' instruction to put out into the deep, Peter (here "Simon") answers: "Master, we toiled all night and took nothing! But at your word I will let down the nets" (5:5). After making an abundant catch Peter falls at Jesus' knees, imploring: "Depart from me, for I am a sinful man, O Lord" (5:8b). Significantly, Jesus uses the singular pronoun to address the following mission to Simon: "Do not be afraid; henceforth you will be catching human beings" (5:10b).

Subsequent to the passage highlighting Peter's call Luke presents an extended number of scenes in which Peter speaks out prominently and others in which he is portrayed as a member of Jesus' inner circle of disciples. After the angels and Simeon, Peter is the first to confess that Jesus is "the Christ of God" (9:20). Along with James and John, but in a more engaged way than these others, Peter is privileged to be with Jesus at the time of his transfiguration. In these latter episodes Luke refers to him as "Peter." He actually receives this name at 6:13-16 when Jesus designates him, his brother, and ten others as "apostles."

Peter is the first apostle on Luke's list. For readers at Philippi who may be very familiar with Paul's firm protestations that he himself is an apostle second to none, Luke's explanation of how Peter came to be an apostle may well have been of more than passing interest. Whatever the Philippian Christians knew about the various facets of this topic of apostleship before the arrival of Luke's Gospel, in it they now receive a clear explanation of Jesus' initiative in calling Peter and then in naming him as one of his twelve apostles.

As they progressed through Luke's narrative, paradigmatic readers at Philippi may have seen a logical connection between Jesus' selection of twelve apostles and the important promise Luke's Jesus makes to these apostles at the time of the Last Supper. Luke includes two additional points regarding Peter and the others before the passage in which they are promised a stellar future ministry. The first is that Jesus entrusted Peter and John with the preparations for the supper (22:8). The second is that Peter and John, along with the others present at the supper, fall into a scandalous dispute (22:24-27) over which of them is to be regarded as the greatest.

After instructing them once again about the imperative of service and humility, Jesus proceeds to commend the apostles for their perseverance and indicates the blessed future they will have. A key element of this future blessedness is that they will "sit on thrones judging the twelve tribes of Israel" (22:30b).

Having made this promise, Jesus then adverts to the obstacle that Satan poses to its fulfillment and indicates to Peter that Jesus intends him to play a pivotal role in thwarting Satan's designs. Addressing him twice as "Simon,

Simon" Jesus then relates that Satan desired to have all the apostles so that he might sift them like wheat. To counter this threat Jesus has prayed for Peter personally so that he will not fail in his own faith. Then, once Peter has turned, he will have the role of strengthening the others (22:31-32). As paradigmatic readers at Philippi will eventually discern, this prediction will be partially fulfilled within the narrative but will await a more complete fulfillment outside the boundaries of the narrative.

Peter's response at this point is bold: "Lord, I am ready to go with you to prison and to death" (22:33). However, from this zenith Luke now portrays Peter falling downward to his nadir. Jesus' words predict this fall: "I tell you, Peter, the cock will not crow this day until you three times deny that you know me" (22:34).

Peter then proceeds to deny Jesus three times. This highly personal breaking of his allegiance to Jesus is underscored by Luke's report that Jesus turns his gaze toward Peter just as the cock crowed. Peter then departs, weeping bitterly. Seemingly he does not renew himself so as to witness at Jesus' cross. His denials thus represent his final words in testimony to Jesus until after the Resurrection—unless Luke's word "acquaintances" is read to signal this apostle's distant presence.

In Luke's resurrection narratives, readers at Philippi find confirmation for something they already knew from I Corinthians, namely that the risen Jesus' first appearance to Peter was his first appearance to an apostle (Luke 24:34; within the same temporal framework Jesus also appears to the disciples traveling to Emmaus). In Luke this appearance is particularly significant because it enables Peter to complete his "turning" and to begin his ministry of "strengthening the brethren."

As Luke's Gospel closes, Peter is, by reason of his personal encounter with Jesus as well as his presence for Jesus' appearance to the larger group of apostles and disciples in Jerusalem, positioned well for the ministries Jesus has indicated for him in numerous instances of external predictive prolepsis. By Jesus' mandate Peter shares in the ministry of preaching repentance and the forgiveness of sins in Jesus' name to all nations (24:47). Peter and the others are indeed to be "witnesses of these things" (24:48), sometimes testifying "before kings and governors" for the sake of Jesus' name (21:12).

To a degree not specified, Peter himself presumably continues to be "a fisher for human beings" (5:10). Certainly he is a brother who will continue to "strengthen his brethren" because he himself has been "turned" by Jesus' prayers (22:32). Finally, along with the other apostles Peter has a role that extends far beyond the end of the narrative. According to Jesus' assignment (22:29-30), his apostles are destined to be seated as judges over the twelve tribes of Israel.

C. *The Arrival of Matthew's Gospel at Philippi*

Matthew's readers at Philippi first encounter Peter at 4:18-22, well after Matthew's narrative has already established a number of points relative to Jesus and his mission. Peter and his brother Andrew are the first disciples Jesus calls. They are called to be "fishers of human beings" and begin to accompany Jesus in his teaching, preaching, and healing from this point forward. During the course of this unfolding journey Matthew portrays Jesus visiting Peter's home and healing his mother-in-law (8:14-15). Then, when Jesus sends forth twelve of his disciples on their own mission, Matthew places Peter at the head of this list, identifying him with these words: "first, Simon who is called Peter" (10:2). At this juncture Matthew does not indicate any interpretation for the name "Peter," nor does he explain his reference to this group of twelve as "apostles."

After portraying Peter so positively, Matthew then evolves a series of sequences in which Peter follows the pattern of success, failure, and restoration. This pattern in Matthew's portrayal of Peter may not have been immediately evident to many readers/hearers at Philippi. Nevertheless, for readers committed to multiple re-readings of the text such a pattern gradually becomes apparent. As part of their reading process the Philippian Christians encounter Matthew's portrayals of Peter as an outspoken disciple in such passages as 15:15; 17:24-27; 18:21; and 19:27. Indeed, because it depicts Peter's wrong answer regarding Roman taxes, Matthew 17:24-27 might well have been especially interesting in the highly Romanized setting of Philippi. In addition to engaging with the meaning of individual passages such as this one, paradigmatic readers at Philippi also engage with the general patterns by which Matthew traces out Peter's trajectory.

Presumably such readers would grasp the pattern of success, failure, and restoration as it is manifested in Matthew's account of Peter walking on water (14:22-32). At least for some distance, by reason of Jesus' invitation, Peter does indeed walk on the water. Yet then his fear and his wavering faith cause him to fail, something that is emphasized to him in Jesus' rebuke: "O man of little faith. . . ." Nevertheless, Peter is restored by Jesus after he desperately calls out: "Lord, save me." He then joins the others in the boat in worshiping Jesus with the acclamation "Truly, you are the Son of God."

As discussed above in chapter 4, Matthew structured his Gospel so that his section on Jesus' public ministry concludes with Peter's confession: "You are the Christ, the son of the living God," and with Jesus' gracious words conferring a new role and new name on Peter (16:13-19). From their reading of 1 Corinthians and Galatians the Philippians knew the names "Cephas" and "Peter." Now, within Matthew's narrative, they encountered

Jesus' powerful logic in bestowing such a name on this disciple. According to Matthew's narrative Jesus intended to establish a "church," and since Simon was Jesus' choice to be the rock foundation for this church, his new name "Peter" signaled his new role. Further, Jesus also entrusted "keys" to him, keys that would enable what Peter bound/loosed on earth to be bound/loosed in heaven.

Beyond reflecting on what the Philippians might have known about Peter's name, it is worth considering what they might have understood to be the meaning of "church." Almost certainly they knew of this term as Paul's designation for the local faith communities he established. This usage is, indeed, reflected in Philippians 4:15 when Paul remarks that "no church" other than the Philippians themselves entered into partnership with him.

But before the arrival of Matthew's Gospel, had the Philippians ever grappled with the more universal meaning of "church?" Clearly, the scope of Jesus' words in Matthew 16:18 cannot be limited to a local community, and Paul himself also references a broader meaning of "church" in Philippians 3:6 when he refers to his past activities as a persecutor of "the church." Still, this question bears repeating: had the Philippian Christians, before their reading of Matthew 16:18, ever considered that the establishment of a "church" was central to Jesus' mission? Also, before their encounter with Matthew 16:18, had the Philippian Christians ever heard that it was Jesus' own strategy to use "Peter" as the foundation for his church?

Peter's confession of Jesus and Jesus' striking affirmation of Peter in response thus constitute a second instance of the Matthean Peter's success. Yet a second failure is not far removed, and it manifests itself when Peter brazenly tries to rebuke Jesus for predicting that his suffering, death, and resurrection are in the offing. Jesus now refers to Peter as "Satan," and instead of being a rock, Peter is now a stumbling block! He is not on the side of God but on the side of human beings.

Pursuing the images of rock and stumbling block, it may now be asked whether the Philippians had previously received any notice from Paul (or from anyone else) regarding Peter's behavior at Antioch as narrated by Paul in Galatians 2:11-14. This question is intriguing on the supposition that Matthew's Gospel did not arrive at Philippi until well after the incident at Antioch. As a review of the relevant passage from Galatians indicates, Peter was, by Paul's account, an obstacle or a stumbling block to Paul's proclamation of the Gospel at Antioch!

What will happen to Peter? As Matthew's narrative unfolds, Jesus again restores him. With James and John he is invited to accompany Jesus to the mount of transfiguration, and while there he is gifted to experience an overwhelming theophany. To this theophany the now restored Peter responds with profound awe.

The third sequence of success, failure, and restoration begins with the bold articulations of his allegiance to Jesus that Peter makes just before Gethsemane: "Though they all fall away because of you, I will never fall away," he proclaims at Matthew 26:33. Then, at 26:35, he avows: "Even if I must die with you, I will not deny you."

Peter's three denials, a crescendo building from the first to the third, represent his third failure—or rather, they are one component of his final failure. The second component emerges from the fact that, despite his bitter weeping, Peter still does not find the means to draw near to Jesus, let alone the courage to die with him. Again, what will happen to Peter? This question is posed from the standpoint of local Christians who may be reading/hearing Matthew's Gospel as the first Gospel to arrive at Philippi.

Jesus, who has previously saved Peter from drowning and has restored him from being "Satan" and a stumbling block, now restores him again, and not Peter solely, but also the other members of the eleven, all of whom are directed by the angel's message, entrusted to the faithful women, to the mountain in Galilee. Then, in the final majestic scene of the Gospel, the risen Jesus draws near to them and commissions them anew.

In effect this final scene of the Gospel functions to restore all eleven of Jesus' apostles to full discipleship. Indeed, the commission now entrusted to them far surpasses in its scope the one Jesus earlier entrusted to them in Matthew 10. It is nothing less than an authorization to make disciples of all nations.

Here Jesus' words represent an instance of external predictive prolepsis that pertains to all of the eleven. Those at Philippi with the capacity to read Matthew paradigmatically recognize that it is one of four predictions in which Peter is grouped with the other members of the eleven. Jesus has previously predicted that they will all suffer persecution, that they will all share in binding and loosing, and that they are all destined to judge the twelve tribes of Israel.

Further, there are two instances of external predictive prolepsis that pertain to Peter alone. He alone is commissioned to hold "the keys of the kingdom" and to be the rock foundation for Jesus' church. Indeed, for paradigmatic readers of Matthew's narrative at Philippi, Peter holds the name "Peter" (or "Cephas") as a continuing sign of the specific role Jesus intends for him to play on behalf of his church.

D. *The Arrival of John's Gospel at Philippi*

In John's Gospel Peter is the third disciple called by Jesus. His brother Andrew brings him to Jesus after telling him: "We have found the Messiah."

Jesus expresses his majestic bearing first by gazing at Peter and identifying him as "Simon, the son of John" (1:42a), and follows this by decreeing to Simon (1:42b): "You shall be called 'Cephas.'" In 1:42c the evangelist explains that this name translates into Greek as "Peter," but he does not provide any explanation of why Jesus deemed it a suitable new name for Simon.

Peter next comes to John's center stage with his confession ending "the Galilean crisis" (6:68-69): "Lord, to whom shall we go? You have the words of eternal life; and we have believed, and have come to know, that you are the Holy One of God." To the extent that paradigmatic readers at Philippi are resonating with such leading concepts of the Gospel of John as "belief," "eternal life," and "remaining," to that extent Peter's auspicious words in this scene resonate positively with them.

Peter's next major interactions with Jesus come in the context of Jesus' proposal to wash his disciples' feet. Peter immediately questions this idea and is not initially moved by Jesus' explanation (13:1-8a). However, after Jesus emphasizes that Peter will have no part in him unless he accepts this gesture, Peter requests to have his hands and head washed as well (13:8b-9).

In this first episode in which both the Beloved Disciple and Peter appear, Peter recognizes the particular closeness this disciple has with Jesus, and he asks the Beloved Disciple to learn from Jesus the identity of the betrayer. The Beloved Disciple is able to gain this piece of information (13:26), but the evangelist does not show him communicating it to Peter. If this episode portrays Peter operating with discretion, the next interaction in which Peter participates shows him returning to his previous style of bold intervention. After he questions Jesus about where he is going, Peter expresses his desire to follow Jesus even at the cost of his life: "Lord, why cannot I follow you now? I will lay down my life for you" (13:37).

Jesus' words, those *preceding* and those *following* Peter's avowal, look to the future. Jesus initially tells Peter: "Where I am going you cannot follow me now; but you shall follow afterward" (13:36b). Subsequently Jesus deflates Peter's bold avowal by declaiming: "Will you lay down your life for me? Truly, truly, I say to you, the cock will not crow till you have denied me three times" (13:38).

These verses contain three instances of predictive prolepsis. Two of Jesus' predictions are fulfilled within the narrative and can be grasped with relative ease by those reading paradigmatically. Yet if the Christians at Philiippi read and re-read Jesus' predictions in light of the remaining chapters of John's Gospel they will gain from John 21 a precise insight as to how Peter will follow Jesus *afterward*. Peter's denials are the obstacle to his following Jesus now, but in John 21 these denials will be overcome so that Peter can follow Jesus through crucifixion.

Peter's denials loom large in John's portrayal of him, yet before these denials John shows him using his sword in Jesus' defense and then trying to follow Jesus into the high priest's courtyard. Jesus expressly condemns Peter's use of the sword (18:11). Nevertheless, paradigmatic readers at Philippi may view Peter's action as following from his earlier declaration that he would willingly lay down his life for Jesus.

The boldness Peter manifests in the garden disintegrates once he is inside the high priest's courtyard. Through his three denials (18:17, 25-27) Peter separates himself from the Good Shepherd, and in effect becomes the hireling who flees at the sight of danger (10:12). In John's portrayal, Peter's failure is unmitigated by any expression of sorrow. After the third denial the cock crows, and Peter simply disappears from the narrative. Peter's disappearance, including his absence from Jesus' cross, is rendered all the more glaring in contrast to the stellar appearance of the Beloved Disciple at the foot of Jesus' cross (19:25-27). (Here it is appropriate to direct attention to the question of how general readers and paradigmatic readers at Philippi are responding to John's portrayal of the Beloved Disciple.)

What will happen to Peter? He has fallen to his nadir and has disappeared from John's story. Nevertheless, Jesus' previous predictions about him are gradually shown to have full validity. Peter reappears in John 20 when Mary Magdalene runs to him and the Beloved Disciple with the news that the stone has been rolled away from Jesus' tomb (20:2). Running back to the tomb, these two disciples assess the arrangement of the burial cloths and the Beloved Disciple (but not yet Peter) comes to believe (20:3-9).

Later that evening Jesus appears to a group of disciples and bestows the Holy Spirit on them, thereby authorizing them to forgive and retain sins (20:22-23). Eight days later Jesus appears to a group of disciples that specifically includes Thomas (20:26-29). Neither Peter nor the Beloved Disciple is explicitly named in either of these scenes, but presumably readers at Philippi consider them to be implicitly present on the basis of their prominent interactions at Jesus' tomb on the morning of the Resurrection.

It is in chapter 21 that John transmits his most positive images of Peter to his readers at Philippi. The Beloved Disciple plays a crucial role in the scene involving the miraculous catch of fish, but from the beginning of this scene to its conclusion Peter is highly prominent (21:4-14). In the abundant success granted to him and to the others in their fishing, is there not the sense of Jesus symbolically entrusting them with a mission for catching others and bringing them to belief?

Whether or not they assess the miraculous catch of fish in reference to a future ministry by Peter and others, paradigmatic readers could not have failed to apprehend what John next conveys regarding Peter's future as the pastor of Jesus' sheep (21:15c, 16c, 17d). Indeed, for such readers the pastoral commission Jesus entrusts to Peter takes on still greater meaning because they read it against the images in John 10 concerning Jesus' own loving care for his sheep.

Further, Peter is now explicitly and poignantly rehabilitated from his egregious denials of Jesus. Not claiming more about his love for Jesus than is warranted, Peter responds steadily to Jesus' test questions. His third and culminating response, "Lord, you know all things, you know that I love you" (21:17), presumably spoke eloquently to the Philippian Christians. Here is a (fragile) disciple who truly loves his Lord. Although he has behaved like a hireling, Peter truly loves Jesus. And Jesus now restores him and entrusts him with the pastoring of Jesus' flock.

Further, just as Jesus the Good Shepherd lays down his life for his sheep (10:11), so also will Peter lay down his own life. What is more, he will give his life precisely in the same external circumstances in which Jesus himself died. For, according to Jesus' prophecy, Peter himself will be crucified! (21:18-19).

Christian readers/hearers living in a Roman colony significantly populated by veterans of the Roman military would have no difficulty grasping the electrifying meaning of these verses. Had any of them previously witnessed or even carried out Roman crucifixions? Even those who had never served in the Roman legions knew full well what crucifixion involved. And now this is what John's Gospel is projecting as its final image of him: Peter crucified! What an inversion of the Roman *cursus honorum* for the disciple Jesus had just commissioned as the pastor of his sheep!

It remains to link the image of Peter crucified with the images Paul projected regarding his own Roman-authorized death at the time when he wrote the letter to the Philippians.[8] In addition to what the Philippian Christians knew about Paul's (*their founder's*) Roman imprisonment and the outcome of his judicial process, these Christians now knew from John's Gospel that Jesus himself had predicted the death of Peter by Roman crucifixion.

This point is of some consequence, for it is not the case that Peter is to die a natural or accidental death. Rather, Jesus indicates that a Roman cross lies in Peter's future. And in a way that is comparable to the attitude of Paul in Philippians, the Johannine Peter graciously accepts the scandalous form of death that is predicted for him. (He only wonders about what is in store for the Beloved Disciple.)

4. Concluding Reflections

For the first time in this study it is now appropriate to note, very briefly, the similarities among the four Gospels and to formulate a concluding conjecture regarding the impact of these narratives at sites in the Roman world beyond Philippi.

When first-century paradigmatic readers (and twenty-first-century paradigmatic readers) read each Gospel for what it discloses regarding Peter, basic points of similarity emerge. In each Gospel Jesus takes particular care in calling Simon and in each Gospel he assigns him the name "Peter." In each Gospel Peter plays a distinctive role within Jesus' ministry, intervening and speaking far more often than any other disciple. In each Gospel the responses given by Peter serve to advance the overall plot of the Gospel as it relates to Jesus' mission, and in each Gospel there is a "subplot" concerning the outcome for Peter himself.

In each Gospel Jesus predicts Peter's failure, and in each narrative Peter fulfills this *internal* prediction of Jesus by notoriously denying Jesus three times and failing to appear at Jesus' crucifixion. (Mark and Matthew narrate an earlier significant failure by Peter for which Jesus labels him "Satan." In both these narratives Jesus' subsequent invitation for Peter to witness his transfiguration restores his standing.) Nevertheless, Peter is rehabilitated before the ending of each Gospel. Further, each Gospel contains *external* predictions in which Jesus envisions positive future endeavors for Peter as a member of the group of Jesus' disciples, but also as an individual disciple.

Among the four Gospels, Mark's is the most reserved in terms of what Jesus predicts for Peter beyond the ending of the narrative. As a member of the group of Jesus' disciples, he will face persecution. As a member of the group of Jesus' disciples, but as the only disciple mentioned by name, he will begin anew "with Jesus" in Galilee. Within the narratives of Luke, Matthew, and John, Peter is named in numerous external predictions. He receives many of these predictions as a member of the group of Jesus' disciples, but Jesus also assigns certain ministries that are peculiar to him.

Thus in Luke's account Jesus assigns solely to Peter the ministry of "strengthening the brethren." In Matthew, Jesus commissions Peter alone to be the rock foundation for Jesus' church and the keeper of the keys of the kingdom. In John, Jesus decisively rehabilitates Peter from his status as a hireling and authorizes him to serve as the good shepherd for Jesus' sheep. Further, Peter will lay down his life through the specific death of Roman crucifixion.

The preceding sections of this chapter have conjectured that these four distinctive portrayals of Peter would, to varying degrees, have resonated positively with the members of the Christian community at Philippi. When these Gospels reached other Pauline and non-Pauline churches that were networked in the Christian movement of the first century, would their impact have been substantially the same? For example, consider the arrival of each

Gospel into the Christian communities addressed by Paul in his Letter to the Galatians. As another example, reflect on the arrival of Mark's Gospel into the location from which John's Gospel was authored.

Because of the many variables and uncertainties pertaining to such situations, caution is clearly in order. Nevertheless, the final conjecture of this study is that, in the province of Galatia and in a wide variety of first-century Christian locations, paradigmatic readers and the other readers/hearers of each Gospel gained a positive appreciation for fearful Peter. For, fundamentally, *each Gospel* provided its readers with significant reasons for viewing Peter favorably. More specifically, *each Gospel* supplied the compelling rationale that Jesus himself had decisively chosen to regard Peter with noteworthy favor.

APPENDIX

Peter's Speech in Each of the Four Gospels

Peter's Speech in Mark:

1. "You are the Christ." (8:29)
2. "Master, it is well that we are here; let us make three booths, one for you and one for Moses and one for Elijah." (9:5)
3. "Lo, we have left everything and followed you." (10:28)
4. "Master, look! The fig tree which you curse has withered." (11:21)
5. "Tell us, when will this be, and what will be the sign when these things are all to be accomplished?" (13:3; with James, John, and Andrew)
6. "Even though they all fall away, I will not." (14:2)
7. "If I must die with you, I will not deny you." (14:3)
8. "I neither know nor understand what you mean." (14:68)
9. "I do not know this man of whom you speak." (14:71)

Peter's Speech in Luke:

1. "Master, we toiled all night and took nothing! But at your word I will let down the nets." (5:5)
2. "Depart from me for I am a sinful man, O Lord." (5:8)
3. "Master, the multitudes surround you and press upon you." (8:45)
4. "The Christ of God." (9:20)
5. "Master, it is well that we are here; let us make three booths, one for you and one for Moses and one for Elijah." (9:33)
6. "Lord, are you telling this parable for us or for all?" (12:41)

7. "Lo, we have left our homes and followed you." (18:28)
8. "Lord, I am ready to go with you to prison and death." (22:33)
9. "Woman, I do not know him." (22:57)
10. "Man, I am not." (22:58)
11. "Man, I do not know what you are saying." (22:60)

Peter's Speech in Matthew:

1. "Lord, if it is you, bid me come to you on the water." (14:28)
2. "Lord, save me." (14:30)
3. "Explain this parable to us." (15:15)
4. "You are the Christ, the son of the living God." (16:16)
5. "God forbid, Lord! This shall never happen to you." (16:22)
6. "Lord, it is well that we are here; if you wish, I will make three booths here, one for you and one for Moses and one for Elijah." (17:4)
7. "Yes." (17:25)
8. "From others." (17:26)
9. "Lord, how often shall my brother sin against me, and I forgive him? As many as seven times?" (18:21)
10. "Lo, we have left everything and followed you. What then shall we have?" (19:27)
11. "Though they all fall away because of you, I will never fall away." (26:33)
12. "Even if I must die with you, I will not deny you." (26:35)
13. "I do not know what you mean." (26:70)
14. "I do not know the man." (26:72)
15. "I do not know the man." (26:74)

Peter's Speech in John:

1. "Lord, to whom shall we go? You have the words of eternal life; and we have believed, and have come to know, that you are the Holy One of God." (6:68-69)

2. "Lord, do you wash my feet?" (13:6)
3. "You shall never wash my feet." (13:8)
4. "Lord, not my feet only but also my hands and my head." (13:9)
5. "Tell us of who it is of whom he speaks." (13:24)
6. "Lord, where are you going?" (13:36)
7. "Lord, why cannot I follow you now? I will lay down my life for you." (13:37)
8. "I am not." (18:17)
9. "I am not." (18:25)
10. "I am going fishing." (21:3)
11. "Yes, Lord; you know that I love you." (21:15)
12. "Yes, Lord; you know that I love you." (21:16)
13. "Lord, you know all things; you know that I love you." (21:17)
14. "Lord, what about this man?" (21:21)

ENDNOTES

Chapter One

1. For example, Oscar Cullmann, *Peter: Disciple, Apostle, Martyr* (London: SCM, 1953); Raymond Brown, et al., *Peter in the New Testament* (Minneapolis: Augsburg, 1973); Terence Smith, *Petrine Controversies in Early Christianity* (Tübingen: Mohr Siebeck, 1985); Pheme Perkins, *Peter, Apostle for the Whole Church* (Columbia: University of South Carolina Press, 1994); Timothy Wiarda, *Peter in the Gospels: Pattern, Personality and Relationship* (Tübingen: Mohr Siebeck, 2000); Christfried Böttrich, *Petrus. Fischer, Fels und Funktionär*. Biblische Gestalten 2. (Leipzig: Evangelische Verlagsanstalt, 2001); Joachim Gnilka, *Petrus und Rom* (Freiburg: Herder, 2002); Fred Lapham, *Peter: The Myth, the Man and the Writings*. JSOTSup 239 (Sheffield: Sheffield Academic Press, 2003).

2. See Mark Allan Powell, *What Is Narrative Criticism?* (Minneapolis: Fortress Press, 1990) for chapters discussing character, setting, and events. Powell includes a discussion of plot within his chapter on events. For a useful reflection on the larger project of narrative criticism see Werner Kelber, "Narrative as Interpretation and Interpretation of Narrative: Hermeneutical Reflections on the Gospels, *Semeia* 39 (1987) 107–33.

3. Mark Stibbe, *John as Storyteller: Narrative Criticism in the Fourth Gospel* (Cambridge: Cambridge University Press, 1992), 17–29, discusses these techniques along with others such as *inclusio* and chiasmus that are especially favored by John. See also pp. 10–19 in Stibbe's fine narrative commentary, *John. Readings: A New Biblical Commentary* (Sheffield: JSOT Press, 1993). The analysis below will identify important instances in which these three techniques enable Mark, Luke, and Matthew, as well as John, to advance their respective narratives.

4. In the next chapter it will be seen that Peter's key role within Mark's plot renders him the most significant character after Jesus. Peter is similarly prominent in the plots of Luke, Matthew, and John. This does not mean that Mark discloses a great deal about Peter's character traits, for as Stephen Smith, *A Lion With Wings: A Narrative-Critical Approach to Mark's Gospel* (Sheffield: Sheffield Academic Press, 1996) 92, points out, Peter is primarily a "functional character" for Mark. With respect to Peter's prominence in John's Gospel, note the following assessment by Alan Culpepper, *Anatomy of the Fourth Gospel: A Study in Literary Design*. (Philadelphia: Fortress Press, 1983) 120: "Next to Jesus, Peter is the most complex character."

5. See Daniel Marguerat and Yvan Bourquin, *How to Read Bible Stories* (London: SCM, 1999) 40–59, for a thorough discussion of the elements in a plot and the various types of plot. Also see Petri Merenlahti's chapter, "The Gospel as a Plot" in his *Poetics for the Gospels? Rethinking Narrative Criticism* (London: T & T Clark, 2002) 99–111.

6. Merenlahti, *Poetics*, 99–100, discusses various understandings of plot, including G. Prince's conception of plot as "the very intelligibility of the narrative."

7. Helpful analyses of Jesus' unfolding mission are given by David Rhoads et al., *Mark as Story* (2d ed. Minneapolis: Fortress Press, 1999); Robert Tannehill, *The Narrative Unity of Luke-Acts A Literary Interpretation. Volume One: The Gospel According to Luke* (Philadelphia: Fortress Press, 1986); Jack Dean Kingsbury, *Matthew as Story* (2d ed. Philadelphia: Fortress Press, 1988); Culpepper, *Anatomy of the Fourth Gospel*; Mark Stibbe, *John.*

8. These categories of time are used by Smith, *A Lion with Wings* 136–37, who derives them from Gerard Genette, *Narrative Discourse: An Essay in Method* (Ithaca: Cornell University Press, 1980), especially 215–22.

9. See Genette, *Narrative Discourse*, 67–79, for amplification on the distinctions between internal and external prolepses. Adele Reinhartz, "Jesus as Prophet: Predictive Prolepses in the Fourth Gospel," *JSNT* 36 (1989) 3–16, at 3–4, illustrates these two types of prolepses with reference to the Gospel of John.

10. Smith, *A Lion with Wings*, 188–89, effectively relates the concept formulated by Genette to the narrative of Mark's Gospel. Here Smith uses Genette's distinction between "the time of narrating" and the time of the story-world.

11. James Ressequie, *The Strange Gospel: Narrative Design and Point of View in John* (Leiden: Brill, 2001) 61–63, analyzes the ways in which John uses these and other types of settings to advance the meaning of his narrative. Daniel Marguerat and Yvan Bourquin, *How to Read Bible Stories*, 79–80, consider "time" as an aspect of "setting" and illustrate how "mortal time," "monumental time," and "metaphorical time" all have importance within Mark's narrative.

12. See Mark Stibbe, *John as Storyteller*, 26–27, for important insights regarding the relationship between structure and plot.

13. Arthur Maynard, "The Role of Peter in the Fourth Gospel," *NTS* 30 (1987) 531–48, at 532. Also Arthur Droge, "The Status of Peter in the Fourth Gospel: A Note on John 18:10-11," *JBL* 109 (1990) 307–11, at 308.

14. While Luke's preface makes it clear that he was influenced by the accounts of others, the present study refrains from any affirmation that Mark's Gospel is one of Luke's sources.

15. My analysis of Luke's desire to testify to Jesus and to encourage committed discipleship (especially vis-à-vis the Roman authorities) is made in Richard Cassidy, *Society and Politics in the Acts of the Apostles* (Maryknoll, NY: Orbis, 1987) 158–60. I would argue similarly with respect to Mark's intent and Matthew's. My analysis regarding John's purposes is made in Richard Cassidy, *John's Gospel in New Perspective* (Markyknoll, NY: Orbis, 1992) 80–88.

16. Stibbe, *John*, 128, uses this term to describe sophisticated readers who will grasp the text's subtleties especially on their re-readings of it. Stibbe does not provide any estimate regarding the percentage of John's audience who were sufficiently literate and talented to merit the designation of pararadigmatic reader. Given the low percentage of literates in the general population even within the eastern provinces of the Roman empire, the percentage of paradigmatic readers is probably minuscule. Nevertheless, the narrative subtleties present in all the Gospels testify directly to the evangelists' conviction that there are readers who can grasp these subtleties.

In his classic study William Harris, *Ancient Literacy* (Cambridge: Harvard University Press, 1989) concludes (p. 267) that the overall level of literacy in Italy during the era of Augustus is likely to have been below fifteen percent. In Harris's view (p. 272), within the empire as a whole the level of literacy varied widely from one region to another, with overall literacy in the western provinces unlikely to have reached the range of five to ten percent. Harris also posits a slight decline in the literacy of the Greek-influenced territories of the East during the era of the empire, suggesting (pp. 273–74) that Rome and some Italian cities may in that period have reached the level of literacy earlier achieved by some Greek cities (but, apparently, not higher than fifteen percent). If fifteen percent literacy is the most that can be presumed in the audiences for the Gospels, then clearly the percentage of paradigmatic readers is only a small fraction of that.

Nevertheless, the relationship between oral and aural reading and what Lucretia Yaghian terms "oculiterate reading" should not be neglected. See Yaghian, "Ancient Reading," 202–30, in Richard Rohrbaugh, ed., *The Social Sciences and New Testament Interpretation* (Peabody, MA: Hendrickson, 1996). Yaghian (p. 209) identifies "scribaliterate reading" as a technical form of oculiterate reading that is carried out on behalf of a particular interpretative community. *Conceptually*, Stibbe's paradigmatic readers and Yaghian's scribes who carry out scribaliterate reading seem not far apart.

17. The essays Richard Bauckham has collected for his edited volume, *The Gospels for All Christians: Rethinking the Gospel Audiences* (Grand Rapids: Eerdmans, 1998) in different ways all envision the Gospels as intended for circulation throughout the entire Christian network. Bauckham sets this innovative proposal forward in his own foundational essay, "For Whom Were the Gospels Written?" especially pp. 10–11, 30–31. It is notably amplified upon by Richard Burridge, "About People, by People, for People: Gospel Genre and Audiences," 113–45.

18. Within *The Gospel for All Christians*, Richard Bauckham's essay, "For Whom Were the Gospels Written?" rightly emphasizes (pp. 26–30) that the audiences for the Gospels must not be treated according to the model usually employed in analyses of the audiences for specific Pauline letters.

19. Antioch of Syria is the location favored by virtually all the scholars whose essays are gathered in David Balch, ed., *The Social History of the Matthean Community* (Minneapolis: Fortress Press, 1991). In his own essay, "Conclusion: Analysis of a Conversation," Jack Dean Kingsbury states (p. 264): "In the last decades, Matthean scholars have almost unanimously identified the city of Antioch of Syria as the place where Matthew's Gospel was written and his community was at home." Nevertheless, as Kingsbury himself notes, Alan Segal's paper, "Matthew's Jewish Voice" (pp. 25–29) posits a somewhat broader range of geographic possibilities including a possible location in Galilee. Further, as Robert Gundry argues in "A Responsive Evaluation of the Social History of the Matthean Community in Roman Syria" (pp. 62–67), there is serious difficulty in linking key passages in Matthew's Gospel with the Christian community at Antioch as it is known from other sources.

An example of a Matthean commentator who wishes to hold open the possibility for composition at Caesarea Maritima is Benedict Viviano, in "The Gospel According to Matthew," in Raymond Brown, et al., eds., *The New Jerome Biblical Commentary* (Englewood Cliffs, NJ: Prentice Hall, 1990) 631, and more recently in "Peter as Jesus' Mouth: Matthew 16:13-20 in the Light of Exodus 4:10-17 and Other Models," in Craig Evans, ed., *The Interpretation of Scripture in Early Judaism and Christianity* (Sheffield: Sheffield Academic Press, 2000) 312–41, at 334.

20. Loveday Alexander, "Ancient Book Production and the Gospels," in Richard Bauckham, ed., *The Gospels for All Christians*, 100, amplifies Bauckham's point that the very "writing down" (as distinct from oral performance) of a Gospel implies the crossing of a boundary into the wider audience of those linked within the social network of the Christian movement.

21. Yaghian, "Ancient Texts," emphasizes that the meaning of texts was transmitted to those whose mode of learning was "auralite." She states (p. 211): "In such an environment, 'reading' implies hearing, and the authors of the NT writings wrote for 'readers' ears' (Polybius 6.38.4.4), not merely for their eyes."

22. See the discussion and citation in chapter 4 below.

23. See Cassidy, *John's Gospel*, 2–3, for amplified comments regarding the role of the final author in authorizing the "publication" of the codex or scroll on which the Gospel was written.

24. Joseph Hellerman's chapter, "Preoccupation with Honor and the *Cursus Honorum*," in his *Reconstructing Honor in Roman Philippi: Carmen Christi as Cursus Pudorum* (Cambridge: Cambridge University Press, 2005) 34–63, elaborates on the pervasive presence of this concern with honor.

25. David Rhoads, "Narrative Criticism: Practices and Prospects," in David Rhoads, ed., *Characterization in the Gospels: Reconceiving Narrative Criticism* (Sheffield: Sheffield Academic Press, 1999) 273, envisions reception criticism as a form of literary criticism that can serve as a complement to narrative criticism.

Chapter Two

1. See Francis Moloney, *The Gospel of Mark* (Peabody, MA: Hendrickson, 2002) 348–52, for a nuanced analysis of the fear that Mark attributes to the women in 16:8 in light of the fear Mark regularly attributes to the male disciples of Jesus within the Gospel proper. At the end of his analysis Moloney correctly assesses that the women's fear does not constitute a decisive barrier regarding the messenger's announcement. Just as Jesus' other predictions are shown to come true, so is it Mark's sense that his prediction in 14:28 will also come true.

2. While the presentation that follows concerning Jesus and his mission is fundamentally my own, I am greatly indebted to the insights of such scholars as Werner Kelber, *Mark's Story of Jesus* (Philadelphia: Fortress Press, 1979); Robert Tannehill, "The Gospel of Mark as Narrative Christology," *Semeia* 16 (1979) 57–97; and David Rhoads, et al., *Mark as Story* (2nd ed. Minneapolis: Fortress Press, 1999). The analyses these three works respectively provide of Jesus' disciples in Mark have also influenced my own presentation in section three below. Note, however, that these studies tend to "blend" Peter into the larger group of disciples to such a degree that Mark's specific emphases regarding Peter are neglected. In my own analysis, Mark traces out a distinctive "sub-plot" that specifically focuses on Peter.

3. Among the helpful analyses of Peter in Mark's Gospel are Timothy Wiarda, "Peter in the Gospel of Mark," *NTS* 45 (1999) 19–37; Ernest Best, "Peter in the Gospel According to Mark," *CBQ* 40 (1978) 547–58; Joachim Gnilka, *Petrus und Rom* (Freiburg: Herder, 2002) 143–49; Raymond Brown, et al., *Peter in the New Testament* (Minneapolis: Augsburg, 1973) 57–73.

4. Reinhard Feldmeier, "The Portrayal of Peter in the Synoptic Gospels," in Martin Hengel, ed., *Studies in the Gospel of Mark* (Philadelphia: Fortress Press, 1985) 59.

5. The messenger's initial words at 16:7 do indeed fulfill Jesus' prediction about being raised up and going before the disciples to Galilee. However, his concluding words ("there you will see him, as he told you") represent a new instance of external predictive prolepsis, for Mark's narrative ends without the disciples actually seeing Jesus in Galilee.

6. Bastiaan van Iersel, *Mark: A Reader-Response Commentary* (Sheffield: Sheffield Academic Press, 1998) 456, emphasizes the jeopardy in which Peter's final words place him.

7. So Moloney, *The Gospel of Mark*, 309.

8. In his assessment of Mark's ending, Norman Petersen, "When Is the End not the End? Literary Reflections on the Ending of Mark's Narrative," *Int* 34 (1980) 151–66, concentrates almost exclusively on Mark 16:8, stressing the tension that a literal reading of this verse creates with the preceding narrative. Thomas Boomershine and Gilbert Bartholomew, "The Narrative

Technique of Mark 16:8," *JBL* 100 (1981) 213–23, stress the consistency between the narrative technique of Mark 16:8 and the narrative technique Mark uses to end earlier stories within his Gospel. In contrast with the almost exclusive focus of these two studies on 16:8, the present study concentrates on the meaning of 16:7 for the *overall* ending Mark bequeaths to his readers.

9. Thomas Boomershine, "Mark 16:8 and the Apostolic Commission," *JBL* 100 (1981) 225–39, at 234–35, analyzes Mark's entire passion/resurrection narrative as a step-by-step fulfillment of Jesus' prophecy at 10:33-34. The emphasis in the present study is that Jesus' prophecy in Mark 14:28 is effectively fulfilled by Mark 16:7. So also Robert Stein, "Mark 14:28 and 16:7," *NTS* 20 (1974), 445–52, who draws attention to the change of tense from Mark 14:28 to Mark 16:7, stating (p. 449): "The change in tenses indicates that what was in the future before the Resurrection (Mark 14:28), i.e., a meeting of Jesus with his disciples in Galilee, is now a present reality for the disciples immediately after the Resurrection." Nevertheless, while the tense change signals that reunion in Galilee is at hand, the disciples and Peter do not actually encounter Jesus before the Gospel ends.

10. Hugh Anderson, *The Gospel of Mark* (Grand Rapids: Eerdmans, 1976) 357, underscores that Mark's wording spotlights Peter here suggesting that an appropriate translation for capturing Mark's emphasis would be: ". . . and Peter in particular."

11. The paragraphs above stress the consistent "preference" Mark's Jesus accords to his highly fallible disciple Peter. Note also the observation by Gnilka, *Peter und Rom*, 146, that Mark achieves an inclusion by having Simon as the first named disciple at 1:16 and Peter as the last named in 16:7. The view of van Iersel, *Mark: A Reader-Response Commentary*, 501, is that because Peter stood out at 14:29 to contradict the prediction Jesus made in 14:27-28, it is appropriate that he be singled out to receive the news that this prediction is now fulfilled. However, in contradicting Jesus at 14:29 Peter does not address the aspect of Jesus' prediction that he will go before the disciples to Galilee. Passing over Jesus' reference to the future after the Resurrection, Peter's response focuses *only* on the fact that *he* (Peter) will not fall away.

Chapter Three

1. Fundamental to the presentation made in this section are Richard Cassidy, *Jesus, Politics, and Society: A Study of Luke's Gospel* (Maryknoll, NY: Orbis, 1978), and idem, "Luke's Audience, the Chief Priests, and the Motive for Jesus' Death," in idem, ed., *Political Issues in Luke-Acts* (Maryknoll, NY: Orbis, 1983) 146–67.

2. Jesus is acclaimed by the Samaritans as "truly the Savior of the world" in John's Gospel at 4:42, the only time that "Savior" appears in Mark, Matthew, or John.

3. See Robert Tannehill's chapter, "Jesus and the Disciples," in his *The Narrative Unity of Luke-Acts: A Literary Interpretation* (Philadelphia: Fortress Press, 1985) 1:203–74, for a highly useful analysis of this topic. Two studies by Charles Talbert are also valuable: "Discipleship in Luke-Acts" in Fernando Segovia, ed., *Discipleship in the New Testament* (Philadelphia: Fortress Press, 1985) 62–75; and "The Way of the Lukan Jesus: Dimensions of Lukan Spirituality," *Perspectives in Religious Studies* 9 (1982) 237–49.

4. A welcome event is the recent publication of the first truly narrative-critical study of Peter in Luke: Yvan Mathieu, *La Figure de Pierre dans L'Œuvre de Luc* (Paris: Gabalda, 2004). Tannehill, *Narrative Unity*, has many significant insights regarding Peter's role in Luke's narrative even though Tannehill is not specifically concerned to trace Peter's "trajectory." Significant insights are also present in Raymond Brown et al., *Peter in the New Testament*

(Minneapolis: Augsburg, 1973) 109–28; Wolfgang Dietrich, *Das Petrusbild der lukanischen Schriften* (Stuttgart: Kohlhammer, 1972); Joachim Gnilka, *Petrus und Rom* (Freiburg: Herder, 2002) 161–69; Josep Rius-Camps, "La Figura de Pedro en la Doble Obra Lucana," 61–99 in Rafael Aguirre Monasterio, ed., *Pedro in la Iglesia Primitiva* (Estrella: Verbo Divino, 1991).

5. Reinhard Feldmeier, "The Portrayal of Peter in the Synoptic Gospels," in Martin Hengel, ed., *Studies in the Gospel of Mark* (Philadelphia: Fortress Press, 1985) 59.

6. There are two instances, both involving direct speech, in which the name "Simon" is used, and there are two significant exceptions to this pattern. Jesus himself addresses this apostle as "Simon, Simon" at 22:31. Subsequently, at 22:34, the eleven relate to the Emmaus disciples that Jesus is risen and that he has appeared to "Simon." See section 4 and n. 17 below for an assessment of the linkage between these two uses of "Simon."

7. Employing his own translation of Jesus' words, Tannehill, *Narrative Unity*, 205, correctly emphasizes the significance of this reply for Peter's future: "Jesus' statement to Simon, 'From now on you will be catching people alive' is both a promise and a task for the future. It is an indication to the readers of Peter's role in the following narrative. However, Peter will not begin his task immediately. Further developments must take place and serious problems must be faced before Peter can enter fully into his appointed role."

8. Mathieu, *La Figure de Pierre*, 90 notes that these are the only two instances in which Luke positions Jesus on a mountain, and discerns a number of correspondences in the two scenes.

9. Joseph Fitzmyer, *The Gospel According to Luke*. 2 vols. AB 28, 28A (New York: Doubleday, 1981–1985) 2:1422, points out that Jesus has just commended the apostles for persevering with him in the trials of his ministry and now makes it clear to Peter that that fidelity is to be further tested.

10. I wish to acknowledge the assistance I was given for the interpretation of this passage on St. Luke's Day, October 18, 2005.

11. Howard Marshall, *The Gospel of Luke* (Grand Rapids: Eerdmans, 1978) 823, adverts to the possibility of irony here. So also Fitzmyer, *The Gospel of Luke*, 2:1425.

12. Mathieu, *La Figure de Pierre*, 169, speaks in terms of Simon "becoming" Peter (living the meaning of his name) in his future relationships with other apostles and disciples.

13. Settimo Cipriani, in Francisco Uricchio, ed., *Pietro nella Sacra Scritura* (Firenze: Citta di Vita, 1975) 95, terms Satan's petition a "counter" prayer. More precisely, Jesus' prayer to the Father "counters" the demand that Satan has already set forth.

14. Rudolf Pesch, *Simon-Petrus* (Stuttgart: Hiersemann, 1980) 48, rightly sees Jesus decisively interposing himself between Satan and Simon in a way that highlights Jesus' personal bond with Peter.

15. Tannehill, *Narrative Unity*, 264.

16. Luke 24 makes a significant contribution with respect to Peter's role in the overall plot structure of Luke's Gospel by establishing the completion of Peter's "turning" and his decisive role in the "strengthening" of the other apostles. Mathieu's statement that "the more one advances in Luke 24, the more the role of Peter diminishes" (*La Figure de Pierre*, 166, 337) does not take appropriate account of these developments in Luke's plot.

17. Tannehill, *Narrative Unity*, 292–93 suggests that the use of the name "Simon" at 24:34 underscores the turning Jesus predicted at 22:32: "The connection between these two passages is reinforced by the fact that they are the only two places in Luke where Peter is called Simon after the formal indication in 6:14 that Jesus gave Simon a new name. Simon is warned and charged with responsibility in 22:31-32, and he begins to fulfill that responsibility by bearing witness to the risen Jesus before Jesus' other followers."

Chapter Four

1. Jack Dean Kingsbury, *Matthew as Story* (2nd ed. Philadelphia: Fortress Press, 1988) has made a surpassing contribution in systematically exploring the significance of 4:17 and 16:21 for Matthew's narrative of Jesus. The analysis below is largely premised on Kingsbury's approach, with one important modification. As a consequence of treating Matthew's second section under the heading "The Ministry of Jesus to Israel and Israel's Repudiation of Jesus," Kingsbury largely overlooks that Matthew climaxes this part of the Gospel with Jesus' stunning announcement, ". . . I will build my church." It will be shown below that this initiative is of great consequence for any attempt to interpret Jesus' mission in Matthew. This announcement is also highly significant for any interpretation of Peter's portrayal by Matthew.

For an exposition of Matthew's narrative that seeks to appreciate the significance of Jesus' five sermons as well as the key connecting clauses at 4:17 and 16:21 see Bernard Combrink, "The Structure of the Gospel of Matthew as Narrative," *Tyndale Bulletin* 34 (1983) 61–90. Combrink's careful analysis would be strengthened by giving focused attention to Matt 16:17-20 as the final episode in Jesus' ministry before his startling pronouncement in 16:21 that suffering and death now lie ahead for him.

2. Matthew 16:17-19 is treated three times in the present chapter. Here the focus is on Jesus' intention to establish a church. Subsequent analysis will focus on the significance of Jesus' renaming of Peter and then on the new roles Jesus is entrusting to him.

3. Jack Dean Kingsbury, *Matthew as Story*, 129, states effectively: "Because Jesus is the protagonist in Matthew's Gospel, the main storyline concerns him. . . . As those whom Jesus calls to be with him, the disciples, too, have a storyline." Kingsbury's entire analysis regarding Jesus' disciples, pp. 129–45, is highly instructive.

4. Peter speaks directly to Jesus at 14:28, 30; 15:15; 16:16; 16:22; 17:4; 17:25, 26; 18:21; 19:27; 26:33, 35; 26:70, 72, 74. Jesus speaks explicitly to Peter at 14:29, 31; 16:17-18; 16:23; 17:25, 27; 26:34; 26:40.

5. Note that Matthew does not expressly identify the Twelve as a distinct group until Jesus is ready to send them forth on a mission to Israel (10:1-4).

6. This acclamation by all those in the boat, Peter presumably included, means that Peter's confession in 16:16 is not the first disclosure of Jesus' exalted identity. Both these declarations, "truly you are the Son of God" (14:33) and "you are the Christ, the Son of the living God" (16:16), occur as the second part of the Gospel is drawing to a close. After Jesus' identity as "the Son of God" and "the Christ, the Son of the living God" is disclosed, Jesus proceeds to reveal his intention of establishing a church.

7. Note that Matthew "balances" his portrayal of the mother of James and John at 27:56 when he reports her presence at Jesus' cross as one of the women who had followed him from Galilee, ministering to him.

8. The predictions of 26:31 and 26:32 are internal to Matthew's narrative; 28:16-20 in effect fulfills the prediction of a reunion in Galilee.

9. To my knowledge the present study is the first to concentrate on Matthew's portrayal of Peter as a significant "subplot" within his larger story of Jesus. See Jack Dean Kingsbury, "The Figure of Peter in Matthew's Gospel as a Theological Problem," *JBL* 98 (1979) 67–83, and Ulrich Luz's excursus, "Peter in the Gospel of Matthew," in his *Matthew 8–20* (Minneapolis: Fortress Press, 2001) 366–68, for analyses that highlight key aspects of Matthew's portrayal of Peter without attempting to trace Peter's full "trajectory." Also see Joachim Gnilka's treatment of Matthew's Peter in his chapter, "Das Petrusbild der Evangelisten," in *Petrus und Rom* (Freiburg: Herder, 2002) 149–60.

10. Reinhard Feldmeier, "The Portrayal of Peter in the Synoptic Gospels," in Martin Hengel, ed., *Studies in the Gospel of Mark* (Philadelphia: Fortress Press, 1985) 59.

11. On p. 123 of his essay, "Peter as Character and Symbol in the Gospel of Matthew," in David Rhoads, ed., *Characterization in the Gospels: Reconceiving Narrative Criticism* (Sheffield: Sheffield Academic Press, 1993), Kari Syreeni rightly directs attention to the significance of this scene for Matthew's portrayal of Peter.

12. Syreeni, "Peter as Character and Symbol in the Gospel of Matthew," 125, understands Peter's "firstness" in two ways. Peter is the first disciple Jesus has selected and Peter is also first in terms of overall prominence.

13. When the disciples see Jesus walking toward them on the sea they cry out "for fear" (14:26b). Jesus himself addresses their fear in his words of reassurance to them: "Take heart, it is I; *have no fear*" (14:27b; emphasis added). The reappearance of fear, Peter's own fear, then proves to be a decisive development as the scene unfolds.

14. Douglas Hare, *Matthew* (Louisville: John Knox, 1993) 169, adverts to this feature of the passage. As the present study's exposition continues, what will emerge is that Jesus responds positively to Peter's request to join him in walking on the water. Indeed, up to this point in the narrative Matthew's Jesus has steadily expressed benevolence toward his disciples. Although Peter will now be admonished for "little faith," the pattern of Jesus' benevolent initiatives and responses will generally continue until 16:22-23, when Peter tries to dissuade Jesus from following his path toward suffering and death.

15. In contrast, when Peter speaks with comparable boldness at the Last Supper, Jesus immediately counters with the prediction that Peter will fail (26:33-34). In this latter scene Matthew discloses Jesus' knowledge that Peter did not have the capability for accomplishing what he professed to accomplish. The outcome for Peter in the present scene is seemingly more open-ended. The reader is allowed to reckon, at least briefly, with the possibility that Peter will have full success.

16. For a recent bibliography for this passage see Luz, *Matthew 8–20*, 353–54. The approach to bibliography followed earlier by Raymond E. Brown et al., *Peter in the New Testament* (Minneapolis: Augsburg, 1973) is an indication of how large the interpretation of this passage looms within studies of Peter in Matthew. On pp. 173–75 the authors provide seven entries for Matthew's Gospel considered as a whole and twenty-four entries specifically relating to Matthew 16.

17. In his essay, "The Gospel and Culture," in *Collected Works of Eric Voegelin* (Baton Rouge: Louisiana State University Press, 1990) 12:202, Voegelin rightly stresses the role of the Father as the third person in this scene. In divine providence, the Father has selected Peter to be the recipient of this privileged revelation regarding Jesus' identity that is beyond the capacity of flesh and blood. Joseph Ratzinger, *Called to Communion* (San Francisco: Ignatius Press, 1996) 61, contrasts Peter's answer (by divine revelation and not by "flesh and blood") in this passage with his response in the next passage when he attempts to dissuade Jesus from following the path to suffering and execution. In the latter passage Peter's answer *is* by "flesh and blood."

18. Richard France, *Matthew* (Grand Rapids: Eerdmans, 1985) 254, points out that there is no other known use of *Petros* as a personal name before this. In France's view "the feminine word for *rock, petra*, is necessarily changed to the masculine petros (stone) to give a man's name, but the word-play is unmistakable. . . ."

19. Daniel Harrington, *The Gospel of Matthew* (Collegeville: Liturgical Press, 1991) 248, observes that Peter's response could be translated as: "May God be gracious to you, Lord!" Thus until Jesus replies, Peter's response does not seem a grievous undermining of Jesus' calling and mission. Nevertheless, the forcefulness, indeed, the "jugular quality" of Jesus'

rebuke to Peter serves to underscore the central importance that Matthew's Jesus attaches to his embrace of his Passion.

20. See Richard Cassidy, "Matthew 17:24-27—A Word on Civil Taxes," *CBQ* 41 (1979) 571–80, for an explication of Jesus' highly nuanced approach to the question of Roman taxation. From the standpoint of the present study it is important to note that Jesus here moves from a criticism of Peter's answer to acting beneficently on Peter's behalf. To some degree this is a "replication" of the beneficence Jesus manifested after Peter's "little faith" in Matthew 14 and that shown to Peter in Matthew 17 when, in the aftermath of Peter's "satanic" intervention (16:22-23), Jesus still allowed him to share the momentous event of the Transfiguration.

21. John Meier, *Matthew* (Wilmington, DE: Michael Glazier, 1980) 335, interprets Peter's bitter weeping as indicating his immediate repentance. This repentance contrasts favorably with the despair Judas manifests at 27:3-10.

Chapter Five

1. For the analysis of Jesus and his mission in John, the pathbreaking study is Alan Culpepper's *Anatomy of the Fourth Gospel: A Study in Literary Design* (Philadelphia: Fortress Press, 1983), especially 106–12 and 89–97. Mark Stibbe, *John. Readings: A New Biblical Commentary* (Sheffield: JSOT, 1993) should be appreciated as the first full-length commentary on this Gospel from a narrative perspective. Also see Mark Stibbe, *John as Storyteller: Narrative Criticism and the Fourth Gospel* (Cambridge: Cambridge University Press, 1992), especially 96–120 and 148–96. Charles Talbert, *Reading John: A Literary and Theological Commentary on the Fourth Gospel and the Johannine Epistles* (New York: Crossroad, 1992) 63–64, correctly insists that the interpreter of John's narrative must focus on the final text of the Gospel without attempting rearrangements and without setting aside John 21. See also Richard Cassidy, *John's Gospel in New Perspective* (Maryknoll, NY: Orbis, 1992).

2. John's Gospel features positive, neutral, and negative uses of the term "the Jews." When this term is used negatively, it references the alliance of the chief priests and the Pharisees, influenced by Satan, against Jesus. See Cassidy, *John's Gospel in New Perspective*, 40–41 and 106, nn. 3, 4, and 6.

3. Culpepper, *The Anatomy of the Fourth Gospel*, provides a clear, concise overview of Jesus' disciples in his section, "The Disciples," 115–25. Culpepper focuses on the seven disciples who emerge as individuals in the course of the narrative: Andrew, Peter, Philip, Nathanael, the Beloved Disciple, Thomas, and Judas. It will be observed below that John never explicitly indicates whether all seven of these disciples are members of "the Twelve." One explanation for the fact that John never clearly indicates who belongs to the Twelve is that John's Gospel never portrays Jesus instructing the Twelve or sending them forth as a group with a particular mission. Since the Twelve is a group that is not prominent within John's narrative (except for this important reference at 6:67), John is seemingly not concerned to provide precise information about the group's membership. See the discussion by Kevin Quast, *Peter and the Beloved Disciple* (Cambridge: Cambridge University Press, 1987) 22–24.

4. Peter's words are recorded at 6:68-69; 13:6, 8, 9, 24, 36, 37; 18:17, 25; 21:3; 21:15, 16, 17; 21:21. While the Beloved Disciple's consistency in following Jesus is superior to Peter's, this disciple's words are recorded only twice (13:25; 21:7).

5. A comprehensive analysis of the Beloved Disciple is provided by Rudolf Schnackenburg, *The Gospel According to John* (New York: Crossroad, 1990) 3:375–88. See also the relevant

chapters in Quast, *Peter and the Beloved Disciple*. A particularly lucid discussion of the portrayal of the Beloved Disciple at John 21:20-24 is given by George Beasley-Murray, *John* (Waco: Word Books, 1987) 409–15.

6. Talbert, *Reading John*, 195. This disciple's privileged status is further attested when Peter presumes that the Beloved Disciple already knows or will be able to gain from Jesus the identity of the betrayer (13:24b may be read with either meaning).

7. James Resseguie, *The Strange Gospel: Narrative Design and Point of View in John* (Leiden: Brill, 2001) 158.

8. Resseguie, *The Strange Gospel*, 162, notes that the Beloved Disciple's identification of Judas initiates a chain reaction in the narrative.

9. The use of "we" in the third clause of this verse is a complicating factor, but it does not disturb the information presented in the first two clauses. See Cassidy, *John's Gospel in New Perspective*, 116–17, n. 22 for an analysis of the use of the first person plural in the third clause of 21:24.

10. In order of their appearance, the following are significant analyses of Peter in the Gospel of John: Raymond Brown, et al., *Peter in the New Testament* (Minneapolis: Augsburg, 1973) 129–47; Culpepper, *The Anatomy of the Fourth Gospel*, 120–21; Arthur Maynard, "The Role of Peter in the Fourth Gospel," *NTS* 30 (1984) 531–48; Patrick Hartin, "The Role of Peter in the Fourth Gospel," *Neot* 24 (1990) 49–61; Joachim Gnilka, *Petrus und Rom* (Freiburg: Herder, 2005) 168–69; Resseguie, *The Strange Gospel*, 150–55.

11. It may be a part of John's narrative strategy to introduce Peter's new name without supplying any information about it. Henceforth John's readers are invited to formulate their own assessments about the aptness of this name as they continue to read about Peter in the remainder of the Gospel. John's portrayal of Peter in 6:66-69 at the time of the "Galilean crisis" provides the best image of him as possessing rocklike steadiness. In contrast, at the time of his denial Peter is at his nadir in terms of rocklike stability.

12. Within John's narrative "Simon Peter" is used eighteen times and "Peter" alone an additional sixteen times. Significantly, after Jesus renames this disciple, his birth name "Simon" is not used in the narrative until the rehabilitation scene at the end of the Gospel when he is three times addressed as "Simon, son of John" (21:15, 16, 17).

13. Stibbe, *John*, 182–83, helpfully draws attention to the spatial similarities in the settings of the sheepfold (*aulē*) of John 10:1-21, the garden of 18:1-11, and the courtyard (*aulē*) of 18:15-27. He also helpfully illumines the roles of the good shepherd, the thief, and the hireling in John 10 and 18, correctly identifying the denying Peter with the fleeing hireling.

In his analysis of the scene in the high priest's courtyard Stibbe presumes that the anonymous disciple is the Beloved Disciple, focuses on this disciple's role as "*a* shepherd" who walks in and out of the fold (184; emphasis added), and does not explicitly advert to the decisive presence of the Good Shepherd himself, i.e., Jesus. Peter is the hireling here precisely because he is fleeing from any association with the one who is his Good Shepherd.

Resseguie, *The Strange Gospel*, 70, observes that Peter does not flee from the courtyard and believes that this precludes his being identified with the hireling. Nevertheless, in fear for his own life Peter really is fleeing from any association with the Good Shepherd (who is now in the process of laying down his own life). Peter is thus a hireling to the hilt—even though he has not yet left the courtyard!

14. Quast, *Peter and the Beloved Disciple*, 143.

15. Alan Culpepper, *The Gospel and Letters of John* (Nashville: Abingdon, 1998) 248, discusses the nuances of the two Greek words for "love," concluding that they are used interchangeably.

16. For example, at 13:8 Peter has asserted, "You shall never wash *my* feet" and at 13:37 he has emphasized, "*I* will lay down *my* life for you."

17. Cassidy, *John's Gospel in New Perspective*, 74, 115 n. 12.

18. For a careful interpretation of Jesus' renewed mandate that Peter follow him see Beasley-Murray, *John*, 410. For the explication that this "following" now precisely involves Roman martyrdom see Cassidy, *John's Gospel in New Perspective*. 74, 78.

19. Beasley-Murray, *John*, 410.

Chapter Six

1. Among the recent studies shedding concentrated light on Philippi are Charalambos Bakirtzis and Helmut Koester, eds., *Philippi at the Time of Paul and After His Death* (Harrisburg, PA: Trinity Press International, 1998) and Peter Pilhofer, *Philippi: Die erste christliche Gemeinde Europas* (Tübingen: Mohr, 1995).

2. Joseph Hellerman, *Reconstructing Honor in Roman Philippi: Carmen Christi as Cursus Pudorum* (Cambridge: Cambridge University Press, 2005) 69.

3. Loveday Alexander, "Chronology of Paul," in Joel Green and Scott McKnight, eds., *Dictionary of Paul and His Letters* (Downers Grove, IL: InterVarsity, 1992), especially 122–23.

4. A. H. Jones, "The Cities of the Roman Empire," in idem, *The Roman Economy: Studies in Ancient Economic and Administrative History*, ed. P. A. Brunt (Totowa, NJ: Rowman and Littlefield, [1973]) 1–34. See also Andrew Lincoln, *Paradise Now and Not Yet* (Cambridge: Cambridge University Press, 1981) 100.

5. Hellerman, *Reconstructing Honor*, 69–70.

6. Michael Thompson, "The Holy Internet: Communication between Churches in the First Christian Generation," in Richard Bauckham, ed., *The Gospels for All Christians* (Grand Rapids Eerdmans, 1998) 57–60, identifies six positive factors and one negative factor that made it urgent for Christians at different locations to seek communication with one another. Thompson's chart, "'Average' Travel Time (in Days)," 61, provides a helpful fleshing out of the physical time that could be involved for reports about individuals (such as Peter) or for codices or scrolls of the Gospels themselves to travel from one Christian community to another.

7. See Thompson, "The Holy Internet," 49–70, for stimulating conjectures regarding the means by which early Christian texts circulated. Thompson is commendably silent about the locations *from which* the Gospels circulated. In the same volume see also Loveday Alexander, "Ancient Book Production and the Circulation of the Gospels," 71–105.

8. The assessments in this and in the following paragraph reflect the analysis in Richard Cassidy, *Paul in Chains: Roman Imprisonment and the Letters of St. Paul* (New York: Crossroad, 2001) 163–89.

BIBLIOGRAPHY

Alexander, Loveday. "Ancient Book Production and the Gospels." In Richard Bauckham, ed., *The Gospels for All Christians*. Grand Rapids: Eerdmans, 1998, 71–111.

———. "Chronology of Paul." In Joel Green and Scott McKnight, eds., *Dictionary of Paul and His Letters*. Downers Grove, IL: InterVarsity, 1992, 115–22.

Anderson, Hugh. *The Gospel of Mark*. Grand Rapids: Eerdmans, 1976.

Bakirtzes, Charlabamos, and Helmut Koester. *Philippi at the Time of Paul and after his Death*. Harrisburg, PA: Trinity Press International, 1998.

Balch, David, ed. *Social History of the Matthean Community*. Minneapolis: Fortress Press, 1991.

Bartholomew, Gilbert, and Thomas Boomershine. "The Narrative Technique of Mark 16:8." *JBL* 100 (1981) 213–23.

Bauckham, Richard, ed. *The Gospels for All Christians: Rethinking the Gospel Audiences*. Grand Rapids: Eerdmans, 1998.

———. "For Whom Were the Gospels Written?" In idem, ed., *The Gospels for All Christians*. Grand Rapids: Eerdmans, 1998.

———. "Response to Philip Esler." *SJT* 51 (1998) 249–53.

Beasley-Murray, George. *John*. Waco: Word Books, 1987.

Beck, Brian. *Christian Character in the Gospel of Luke*. London: Epworth Press, 1989.

Best, Ernest. "Peter in the Gospel According to Mark." *CBQ* 40 (1978) 547–58.

Bizot, Catherine, and Regis Burnet. *Pierre, l'apotre fragile*. Paris: Desclée de Brouwer, 2001.

Böttrich, Christfried. *Petrus. Fischer, Fels und Funktionär.* Leipzig: Evangelische Verlagsanstalt, 2001.

Boomershine, Thomas. "Mark 16:8 and the Apostolic Commission." *JBL* 100 (1981) 225–39.

Brawley, Robert. *Centering on God: Method and Message in Luke-Acts*. Louisville: Westminster John Knox, 1990.

Brown, Raymond, et al., eds. *Peter in the New Testament*. Minneapolis: Augsburg, 1973.

———. and John Meier. *Antioch and Rome*. New York: Paulist, 1983.

Burridge, Richard. "About People, by People, for People: Gospel Genre and Audience." In Richard Bauckham, ed., *The Gospels for All Christians*. Grand Rapids: Eerdmans, 1998, 113–45.

Cassidy, Richard. *Jesus, Politics, and Society: A Study of Luke's Gospel*. Maryknoll, NY: Orbis, 1978.

———. *John's Gospel in New Perspective*. Maryknoll, NY: Orbis, 1992.

———. "Matthew 17:24-27—A Word on Civil Taxes." *CBQ* 41 (1979) 571–80.

———. *Paul in Chains: Roman Imprisonment and the Letters of Paul*. New York: Crossroad, 2001.

———. *Society and Politics in the Acts of the Apostles*. Maryknoll, NY: Orbis, 1987.

Cipriani, Settimo. "Pietro nei Sinottici." In Francesco Uricchio, ed., *Pietro nella Sacra Scrittura*. Firenze: Citta di Vita, 1975, 69–98.

Cullmann, Oscar. *Peter: Disciple, Apostle, Martyr*. London: SCM, 1953.

Culpepper, Alan. *Anatomy of the Fourth Gospel: A Study in Literary Design*. Philadelphia: Fortress Press, 1983.

———. *The Gospel and Letters of John*. Nashville: Abingdon, 1998.

Crump, David. *Jesus the Intercessor. Prayer and Christology in Luke-Acts*. Grand Rapids: Baker Books, 1999.

Darr, John. *On Character Building: The Reader and the Rhetoric of Characterization in Luke-Acts*. Louisville: Westminister John Knox, 1992.

Dietrich, Wolfgang. *Das Petrusbild der lukanischen Schriften*. Stuttgart: Kohlhammer, 1972.

Droge, Arthur. "The Status of Peter in the Fourth Gospel: A Note on John 18:10-11." *JBL* 109 (1990) 307–11.

Dschulnigg, Peter. *Petrus im Neuen Testament*. Stuttgart: Katholisches Bibelwerk, 1996.

Esler, Philip. "Community and Gospel in Early Christianity: A Response to Richard Bauckham's *Gospels for all Christians*." *SJT* 51 (1998) 235–48.

Evans, Craig, ed. *The Interpretation of Scripture in Early Judaism and Christianity*. London: T & T Clark, 2004.

———, ed. *Early Christian Interpretation of the Scriptures of Israel: Investigations and Proposals*. Sheffield: Sheffield Academic Press, 1997.

Feldmeier, Reinhard. "The Portrayal of Peter in the Synoptic Gospels." In Martin Hengel, ed., *Studies in the Gospel of Mark*. Philadelphia: Fortress Press, 1985, 59–63.

Fishbane, Simcha, ed. *Essays in the Social Scientific Study of Judaism and Jewish Society*. Montreal: Concordia University Press, 1990.

Fitzmyer, Joseph. *The Gospel According to Luke*. 2 vols. AB 28, 28A. New York: Doubleday, 1985.

France, Richard. *Matthew*. Grand Rapids: Eerdmans, 1985.

Genette, Gerard. *Narrative Discourse. An Essay in Method*. Ithaca: Cornell University Press, 1990.

Gnilka, Joachim. *Petrus und Rom: Das Petrusbild in den ersten zwei Jahrhunderten*. Freiburg: Herder, 2002.

Gundry, Robert. *Matthew: A Commentary on His Handbook for a Mixed Church Under Persecution*. Grand Rapids: Eerdmans, 1994.

———. "A Responsive Evaluation of the Social History of the Matthean Community in Roman Syria." In David Balch, ed., *The Social History of the Matthean Community*. Minneapolis: Fortress Press, 1991, 62–67.

Hare, Douglas. *Matthew*. Louisville: John Knox, 1993.

Harrington, Daniel. *The Gospel of Matthew*. SP 1. Collegeville: Liturgical Press, 1991.

Harris, William. *Ancient Literacy*. Cambridge, MA: Harvard University Press, 1989.

Hartin, Patrick. "The Role of Peter in the Fourth Gospel." *Neot* 24 (1990) 49–61.

Hellerman, Joseph. *Reconstructing Honor in Roman Philippi: Carmen Christi as Cursus Pudorum*. Cambridge: Cambridge University Press, 2005.

Hengel, Martin. *Studies in the Gospel of Mark*. Philadelphia: Fortress Press, 1985.

Jones, A. H. "The Cities of the Roman Empire." In idem, *The Roman Economy: Studies in Ancient Economic and Administrative History*, ed. P. A. Brunt. Totowa, NJ: Rowman and Littlefield, 1973, 1–34.

Kelber, Werner. *Mark's Story of Jesus*. Philadelphia: Fortress Press, 1979.

———. "Narrative as Interpretation and Interpretation of Narrative: Hermeneutical Reflections on the Gospels." *Semeia* 39 (1987) 107–33.

Kingsbury, Jack Dean. "The Figure of Peter in Matthew's Gospel as a Theological Problem." *JBL* 98 (1979) 67–83.

———. *Matthew as Story*. 2nd ed. Philadelphia: Fortress Press, 1988.

Lapham, Fred. *Peter: The Myth, the Man and the Writings*. Sheffield: Sheffield Academic Press, 2002.

Lincoln, Andrew. *Paradise Now and Not Yet*. Cambridge: Cambridge University Press, 1981.

Luz, Ulrich. *Matthew 8–20*. Minneapolis: Fortress Press, 2001.

Marguerat, Daniel, and Yvan Bourquin. *How to Read Bible Stories: An Introduction to Narrative Criticism*. London: SCM, 1999.

———. "La Mort d'Ananias et Saphira (Ac 5,1-11) dans la Stratégie Narrative de Luc." *New Testament Studies* 39 (1993) 209–23.

Marshall, Howard. *The Gospel of Luke*. Grand Rapids: Eerdmans, 1978.

Matera, Frank. "The Plot of Matthew's Gospel." *CBQ* 49 (1987) 233–53.

Mathieu, Yvan. *La Figure de Pierre dans L'Œuvre de Luc*. Paris: Gabalda, 2004.

Maynard, Arthur. "The Role of Peter in the Fourth Gospel." *NTS* 30 (1984) 531–48.

Meier, John. *Matthew*. Wilmington, DE: Michael Glazier, 1980.

Merenlahti, Petri. *Poetics for the Gospels? Rethinking Narrative Criticism*. London: T & T Clark, 2002.

Mitchell, Margaret. "Patristic Counter-Evidence to the Claim that 'The Gospels Were Written for All Christians.'" *NTS* 51 (2005) 36–79.

Moloney, Francis. *The Gospel of Mark*. Peabody, MA: Hendrickson, 2002.

Nau, Arlo. *Peter in Matthew; Discipleship, Diplomacy, and Dispraise*. Collegeville: Liturgical Press, 1992.

Perkins, Pheme. *Peter, Apostle for the Whole Church*. Columbia: University of South Carolina Press, 1994.

Pesch, Rudolf. *Simon-Petrus: Geschichte und geschichtliche Bedeutung des ersten Jüngers Jesu Christi*. Stuttgart: Hiersemann, 1980.

Petersen, Norman. "When Is the End Not the End? Reflections on the Ending of Mark's Narrative." *Interp* 34 (1980) 151–66.

Pilhofer, Peter. *Die erste christliche Gemeinde Europas*. Tübingen: Mohr, 1995.

Powell, Mark. *What is Narrative Criticism?* Minneapolis: Fortress Press, 1990.

Quast, Kevin. *Peter and the Beloved Disciple*. Sheffield: JSOT Press, 1989.

Ratzinger, Joseph. *Called to Communion*. San Francisco: Ignatius Press, 1996.

Reinhartz, Adele. "Jesus as Prophet: Predictive Prolepses in the Fourth Gospel." *JSNT* 36 (1989) 3–16.

Resseguie, James. *The Strange Gospel: Narrative Design and Point of View in John*. Leiden and Boston: Brill, 2001.

Rhoads, David, ed. *Characterization in the Gospel: Reconceiving Narrative Criticism*. Sheffield: Sheffield Academic Press, 1999.

Rhoads, David, et al., *Mark as Story*. 2nd ed. Minneapolis: Fortress Press, 1999.

———. "Narrative Criticism and the Gospel of Mark." *JAAR* 50 (1982) 411–33.

Rius-Camps, Josep. "La Figura de Pedro en la Doble Obra Lucana." In Rafael Aguirre Monasterio, ed., *Pedro en la Iglesia Primitiva*. Estrella: Verbo Divino, 1991, 61–99.

Rohrbaugh, Richard, ed. *The Social Sciences and New Testament Interpretation*. Peabody, MA: Hendrickson, 1996.

Sand, Alexander. *Das Evangelium nach Matthäus*. Regensburg: Pustet, 1986.

———. *Das Matthäus-Evangelium*. Darmstadt: Wissenschaftliche Buchgesellschaft, 1991.

Schnackenburg. Rudolf. *The Gospel According to John*. 3 vols. New York: Crossroad, 1990.

Smith, Stephen. *A Lion with Wings: A Narrative-Critical Approach to Mark's Gospel*. Sheffield: Sheffield Academic Press, 1996.

Segal, Alan. "Matthew's Jewish Voice." In David Balch, ed., *The Social History of the Matthean Community*. Minneapolis: Fortress Press, 1991, 3–37.

Segovia, Fernando, ed. *What Is John? Readers and Readings of the Fourth Gospel*. Atlanta: Scholars Press, 1996.

———. *What Is John? Vol. II: Literary and Social Readings of the Fourth Gospel*. Atlanta: Scholars Press, 1998.

Smith, Terence. *Petrine Controversies in Early Christianity: Attitudes Towards Peter in Christian Writings of the First Two Centuries*. Tübingen: Mohr, 1985.

Stein, Robert. "A Short Note on Mark xiv.28 and xvi.7." *NTS* 20 (1974) 445–52.

Stibbe, Mark. *The Gospel of John as Literature: An Anthology of Twentieth-century Perspectives*. Leiden: Brill, 1993.

———. *John. Readings: A New Biblical Commentary.* Sheffield: JSOT Press, 1993.

———. *John as Storyteller: Narrative Criticism in the Fourth Gospel*. Cambridge: Cambridge University Press, 1992.

Syreeni, Kari. "Peter as Character and Symbol in the Gospel of Matthew." In David Rhoads, ed., *Characterization in the Gospels: Reconceiving Narrative Criticism*. Sheffield: Sheffield Academic Press, 1999, 106–52.

Talbert, Charles. "Discipleship in Luke-Acts." In Fernando Segovia, ed., *Discipleship in the New Testament*. Philadelphia: Fortress Press, 1985, 62–75.

———. *Reading John: A Literary and Theological Commentary on the Fourth Gospel and the Johannine Epistles*. New York: Crossroad, 1992.

———. "The Way of the Lukan Jesus: Dimensions of Lukan Spirituality." *Perspectives in Religious Studies* 9 (1982) 237–49.

Tannehill, Robert. *The Narrative Unity of Luke-Acts. A Literary Interpretation Vol. I. The Gospel According to Luke*. Philadelphia: Fortress Press, 1986.

Thiede, Carsten. *Simon Peter: from Galilee to Rome*. Exeter: Paternoster, 1996.

Thompson, Michael. "The Holy Internet: Communication Between Churches in the First Christian Generation." In Richard Bauckham, ed., *The Gospel for All Christians*. Grand Rapids: Eerdmans, 1998, 49–70.

Uricchio, Francesco, ed. *Pietro nella Sacra Scrittura*. Firenze: Citta di vita, 1975.

van Iersel, Bastiaan. *Mark: A Reader-Response Commentary*. Sheffield: Sheffield Academic Press, 1998.

Viviano, Benedict. "The Genres of Matthew 1-2: Light from 1 Timothy 1:4." *Revue Biblique* (1990) 31–53.

———. "The Gospel According to Matthew." In Raymond Brown, et al., eds., *The New Jerome Biblical Commentary*. Englewood Cliffs, NJ: Prentice Hall, 1990, 630–74.

———. "Peter as Jesus' Mouth: Matthew 16.13-20 in the Light of Exodus 4.10-17 and Other Models." In Craig Evans, ed., *The Interpretation of Scripture in Early Judaism and Christianity*. London: T & T Clark, 2004, 312–41.

———. "Where Was the Gospel of Matthew Written?" *Catholic Biblical Quarterly* (1979) 533–46.

Voegelin, Eric. *The Collected Works of Eric Voegelin*, Vol. 12. Ed. Ellis Sandoz. Baton Rouge: Louisiana State University Press, 1989.

Wiarda, Timothy. *Peter in the Gospels; Pattern, Personality and Relationship*. Tübingen: Mohr Siebeck, 2000.

———. "Peter as Peter in the Gospel of Mark." NTS 45 (1999) 19–37.

Yaghian, Lucretia. "Ancient Reading." In Richard Rohrbaugh, ed., *The Social Sciences and New Testament Interpretation*. Peabody, MA: Hendrickson, 1996, 206–30.

INDEX OF BIBLICAL PASSAGES

INDEX OF MODERN AUTHORS